Anne Herrmann

A Menopausal Memoir
Letters from Another Climate

"**W**ith wry grace and a light touch, Anne Herrmann portrays her experience of surgically induced menopause and her entry into mid-life. Letters to significant people in her life offer meditations on embodiment, sexualities, multiple identities, and self-in-relation. Situated in contemporary feminist thought, Herrmann's memoir shows how theory can serve to enlarge our store of available reality. *A Menopausal Memoir* is an engaging book—its pace is fast, its language stylish, its authorial voice compelling."

Jeanne Marecek, PhD
*Professor of Psychology
and Women's Studies,
Swarthmore College,
Swarthmore, PA*

A Menopausal Memoir
Letters from Another Climate

HAWORTH Innovations in Feminist Studies
Esther Rothblum, PhD and Ellen Cole, PhD
Senior Co-Editors

New, Recent, and Forthcoming Titles:

Prisoners of Ritual: An Odyssey into Female Genital Circumcision in Africa
by Hanny Lightfoot-Klein

Foundations for a Feminist Restructuring of the Academic Disciplines
edited by Michele Paludi and Gertrude A. Steuernagel

Hippocrates' Handmaidens: Women Married to Physicians by Esther Nitzberg

Waiting: A Diary of Loss and Hope in Pregnancy by Ellen Judith Reich

God's Country: A Case Against Theocracy by Sandy Rapp

Women and Aging: Celebrating Ourselves by Ruth Raymond Thone

Women's Conflicts About Eating and Sexuality: The Relationship Between Food and Sex
by Rosalyn M. Meadow and Lillie Weiss

A Woman's Odyssey into Africa: Tracks Across a Life by Hanny Lightfoot-Klein

Anorexia Nervosa and Recovery: A Hunger for Meaning by Karen Way

Women Murdered by the Men They Loved by Constance A. Bean

Reproductive Hazards in the Workplace: Mending Jobs, Managing Pregnancies
by Regina Kenen

Our Choices: Women's Personal Decisions About Abortion by Sumi Hoshiko

Tending Inner Gardens: The Healing Art of Feminist Psychotherapy
by Lesley Irene Shore

The Way of the Woman Writer by Janet Lynn Roseman

Racism in the Lives of Women: Testimony, Theory, and Guides to Anti-Racist Practice
by Jeanne Adleman and Gloria Enguidanos

Advocating for Self: Women's Decisions Concerning Contraception
by Peggy Matteson

Feminist Visions of Gender Similarities and Differences by Meredith
M. Kimball

Experiencing Abortion: A Weaving of Women's Words by Eve Kushner

Menopause, Me and You: The Sound of Women Pausing by Ann M. Voda

Feminist Theories and Feminist Psychotherapies: Origins, Themes, and Variations
by Carolyn Zerbe Enns

Celebrating the Lives of Jewish Women: Patterns in a Feminist Sampler edited by Rachel
Josefowitz Siegel and Ellen Cole

Women and AIDS: Negotiating Safer Practices, Care, and Representation edited by Nancy
L. Roth and Linda K. Fuller

A Menopausal Memoir: Letters from Another Climate by Anne Herrmann

Women in the Antarctic edited by Esther D. Rothblum, Jacqueline S. Weinstock,
and Jessica F. Morris

A Menopausal Memoir
Letters from Another Climate

Anne Herrmann

The Harrington Park Press
An Imprint of The Haworth Press, Inc.
New York • London

Published by

The Harrington Park Press, an imprint of The Haworth Press, Inc., 10 Alice Street, Binghamton, NY 13904-1580

The Haworth Press, Inc., 10 Alice Street, Binghamton, NY 13904-1580

Cover design by Marylouise E. Doyle.

The Library of Congress has cataloged the hardcover edition of this book as:

Herrmann, Anne.
    A menopausal memoir : letters from another climate / Anne Herrmann.
       p.   cm.
    Includes bibliographical references.
    ISBN 0-7890-0296-5 (alk. paper)
    1. Herrmann, Anne—Health. 2. Menopause—Biography. I. Title.
RG186.H47   1998
362.1'98175'0092—dc21
[B]   97-31420
                                                        CIP

ISBN 1-56023-919-0 (pbk.)

CONTENTS

Acknowledgments   vii

Chapter 1. Letter to the Reader: Mourning and Memory   1

Chapter 2. Letter to My Mother   13

Chapter 3. Letter to an (Ex-) Lover   27

Chapter 4. Letter to a College Friend   39

Chapter 5. Letter to My Father   51

Chapter 6. Letter to a Gay Man   63

Chapter 7. Letter to (Two) Young Women   77

Chapter 8. Letter to My (God) Mother   89

Chapter 9. Letter to Myself   99

Bibliographic Essay   109

ABOUT THE AUTHOR

Anne Herrmann, PhD, is Associate Professor of English and Women's Studies at the University of Michigan, Ann Arbor. She is the author of *The Dialogic and Difference: "An/Other Woman" in Virginia Woolf and Christa Wolf* (Columbia University Press, 1989) and co-editor, with Abigail Stewart, of *Theorizing Feminism: Parallel Trends in the Humanities and Social Sciences* (Westview Press, 1994). Dr. Herrmann received her BA from Stanford University, a LizPhil from the University of Zürich, and her PhD in Comparative Literature from Yale University.

Acknowledgments

I would like to express my gratitude to those without whose conversations I would not have had the courage to continue with this coming-into-writing and who generously gave of their time as readers and from whose responses I learned much about my own desires and disavowals, as well as how readers always seem to wish from the author a different book: Michael Awkward, Liz Barnes, Johanna Frank, Matt Griffin, Bert Ortiz, Marlon Ross, Abby Stewart, and Martha Umphrey.

I would also like to thank the Office for Vice President for Research (OVPR) at the University of Michigan for providing funds that enabled me to take a term's leave, and to Tricia Ortiz and Ted Alway whose hospitality has given me, at much appreciated intervals, a place to work.

The addressees, who have been chosen not through any willingness on their own part, remain unnamed, and thereby, hopefully unharmed.

The photograph of Samnaun, Switzerland was taken by George Herrmann and the photograph of the Moana Hotel is photographer unknown, printed by courtesy of the Hawaii State Archives.

climacteric

[from Latin, from Greek *klimakter* round of a ladder, from *klimax* ladder]

Relating to, or constituting, a climacteric; critical.

noun.

1. A period or point in human life (as the menopause) in which some great change in the constitution, health, or fortune takes place or is supposedly likely to occur; as, **the climacteric** or **grand climacteric**, one's sixty-third year.

2. Any critical period.

This menopause is probably the least glamorous topic imaginable; and this is interesting, because it is one of the very few topics to which cling some shred and remnants of taboo.

Ursula K. Le Guin

The menopause has not only come of age, it's come out of the closet.

Joanna Goldsworthy

Chapter 1

Letter to the Reader:
Mourning and Memory

Whoever says You does not have something;
he has nothing.
But he stands in relation.

Martin Buber, *I and Thou*

This memoir is the result of memory work—Memory work as the product of mourning. Mourning the loss not of a family member, but a part of the body. Not as body part but as female body. Mourning not a lost potential for motherhood, but of one's body image as female. Same-sex desire as the wish for a female body: one's own as a body that can be narcissistically invested; the mother's, so as to deny her premature and inevitable loss; the other woman's as the body threatened by nonexistence, yet made attainable through the disavowal of its unattainability.

If I speak in terms of loss you will assume I couldn't be mourning the loss of my organs. You will think I must be grieving my childlessness, the fact of its irreversability. You will wonder why recovery is taking so long, since I've never wanted to be a mother anyway.

Why do I need to speak at all?

I lost my mother in my twenties. Recovering from the loss of my ovaries and uterus made me remember, one more time, the loss of her. I imagine an improbable dialogue with her, in the form of a letter. All the letters are to people I have been close to, but not all those who are close to me now appear as addressee.

I am telling you this because how else will you know?

I wrote this memoir as part of a recovery process: from a benign condition that compromised my menstrual cycles for possibly most of my life (endometriosis); from surgery that involved the removal of reproductive organs (hysterectomy and bilateral ooph-orectomy); from an unexpected, premature, and precipitous entrance into menopause. Recovery required recovering the histories of the body/bodies that had been lost from a position of intense isolation within the body. Bodies cannot speak to one another. They require mediation, through the professional purveyor of legitimate medical knowledge, through the laying on of hands by alternative healers, through language.

As a feminist I have spent most of my life thinking about the relationship between bodies, gender identity, and the category of experience, asking, how do we know that what we have had is an experience? As a literary theorist I have thought about what counts as experience and how it enters language, losing its relationship to the real by acquiring the attributes of representation. As the bilingual offspring of (Swiss) immigrants I repeatedly return to the epistolary as a way of both enacting and disavowing the inherent division(s) within language. This memoir is a work of literary nonfiction: nothing I say has been invented, but the form, and thus the meanings, are solely my invention.

Who am I addressing?

I was considered completely well until it was discovered that I had been harboring an illness. For how long, no one will ever know. Because I was suffering from a non-life-threatening condition and not a disease, I could have been living with it for most of my adult life. While never threatening my life, it had largely governed it, affecting a monthly cycle whose pain and affective volatility I had learned to manage with determination and discipline over the course of thirty years. Because the condition can be diagnosed only when observable to the human eye, it requires surgical intervention, in its least intrusive form as laparoscopy.

Eliminating the symptoms *(which I had in the form of a diagnosable condition only for as long as it took to remove its cause on the operating table)* requires the cessation of the menstrual cycle through the removal of both ovaries. Without the ovaries the risk for uterine cancer increases, thereby medically mandating the removal of the uterus. This induces instant menopause and precipitated me, without anticipation or preparation, into middle age. Initiated under anesthesia, menopause lasted for as long as I was estrogen deprived. Since the condition is known to be estrogen dependent, I was advised to defer HRT (Hormone Replacement Therapy) for at least three months. At forty-three, on HRT, I have finished menopause and have barely begun to understand middle age. I have lost the organs, not vital ones, that from an early age I never intended to use.

No one will ever know how long I suffered from endometriosis or what it can be held accountable for. That can only be reconstructed in the form of a "coming-out" story: the condition that was always present but never recognized that retrospectively makes sense of almost everything. Once called the "career woman's disease," it is more common among those who defer child-bearing but is taken seriously only when it leads to infertility. Endometriosis occurs when the lining of the uterus attaches itself to nearby organs—ovaries, bowel, urinary tract—instead of moving out of the uterus with the menstrual flow. No one knows why this happens. Like any other endometrial tissue, it bleeds every month, potentially causing severe pain. Unlike other diseases, the severity of the symptoms are no indication of the amount of endometrial tissue present: very little tissue can cause immense pain; the severest case can result in only sporadic symptoms. The most common symptom is extremely painful menstrual periods.

But what criteria are there for distinguishing between normal and abnormal menstrual pain, or, for that matter, between any normal and abnormal discomfort associated with the female body? How is one to differentiate between a life governed by (as opposed to) tyrannized by a monthly cycle? Because the potential for reproduction remains the focus when treating the female body medically, any anomaly or abberation will necessarily be made subordinate to it. Even if never exercised, that possibility remains the difference that constructs sexual difference, at least gynecologically. This is why being unable to bear children is not a reason not to have them in some other way, and this is why not wanting children does not make this a tale not to be told.

I can't remember my periods ever not being painful, although over a lifetime they became normalized through increasingly powerful painkillers. Occasionally, as an adolescent, a summer month would pass without my realizing that I had forgotten to take some form of medication. But that was a rare occurrence and eventually a nonexistent one. In high school I remember taking a taxicab home every month *(after the nurse received permission from one of my parents, usually my father, since he was more likely to be in his office)* to spend the afternoon writhing on the bed due to the ineffectiveness of Midol. By dinnertime the acute pain had subsided, leaving me to feel as though I had just arisen from a sickbed. *I remember standing in front of the Chicago Art Institute when my mother told me that my (menstrual) pain bestowed a certain beauty. Another time, years later, she and I turned around on the way to San Francisco because the pain had become so unbearable and I spent the drive home groaning in the backseat. Did her irritation stem from the fact that we had missed Judy Chicago's "Dinner Party" or from her concern about my condition?* Recently a colleague in the Women's Studies program mentioned that she could always tell when I was menstruating because, in spite of the medication, the pain could be read all over my face.

Several years ago I began experiencing additional discomfort between periods. During certain months the bloating was so severe I could barely eat; at times I even found it difficult to walk. Then one month the pain persisted. My period came and went but the discomfort had failed to disappear. I went to see a doctor. I gave her a medical history that included two different but interrelated narratives. The first involved severe bloating that once precipitated me out of a collegewide meeting into the emergency room, where they sent me home with a stool softener and antacids. *On the way there a student found me in tears running across campus. He offered to accompany me, parked the car, and eventually took me home for homemade chicken soup.* The second narrative involved an episode that had begun several years earlier. Approximately once a year I would be stricken suddenly by the most intense abdominal pain, causing me to heave and writhe on the floor. While the acute pain subsided almost as quickly as it came, the effect was so debilitating that I would spend several days in bed, unable to stand up straight. Since I don't have to appear in an office every day and these episodes seemed not to coincide with the days I taught, they never interfered with work performance and thus were not considered dysfunctional. These episodes have since been attributed to the rupturing of ovarian cysts (known to be excruciatingly painful). I would mention them to various gynecologists during my annual visits, but they either did not respond or took copious notes or told me to come back during one of the episodes.

Because I had once visited a PMS clinic I kept close track of my menstrual cycle on a PMS chart which led me to observe that these bouts always occurred several days after ovulation. I mentioned this to the two male interns in the emergency room who showed no interest. But my family practitioner said it was the clue that led her to request the ultrasound that led me to the gynecologist who eventually performed the surgery.

The report from the radiologist on the ultrasound came back as follows:

> *Findings:* There are bilateral hypoechoic ovarian cyst lesions. These contain low-level echoes as well as focal

nodular areas of tissue within the cysts. The maximal dimension of the largest left-sided cyst is 4.4 cm and that of the right 3.5 cm. The uterus is normal and no free fluid is seen.

Impression: In a premenopausal woman the possibilities include endometriosis, PID-related diseases, hemorrhagic ovarian cysts and neoplasm.

My ensuing discussions with the gynecologist revolved around what kinds of cysts these were, an elevated CA 125 blood count, and the amount of pain I regularly experienced. All the numbers were right in the middle, she said. The cysts were large, but not dangerously so, not over 5 cm. The CA 125 was elevated, but far from the numbers of those with diagnosed ovarian cancer. Even my age. Had I been younger she would have said, "Let's wait and see." Had I been older, she might have encouraged surgery. All the evidence, including the fact that I was symptomatic, pointed in the direction of endometriosis.

The two options presented to me were surgery, which I had never experienced before, or medication. In my case, it was Lupron, a drug that induces instant menopause *(which I had never thought about except in connection with my mother, who had died fifteen years earlier).* Apart from side effects such as hot flashes, joint aches, and insomnia, if taken longer than six months Lupron begins to bring on osteoporosis. There was, of course, a third option, which was to do nothing. Since I only had these debilitating bouts about once a year, I could just live with them, she said. But then there was my age, too much "in the middle," to not do anything at all.

For two weeks I worked on arriving at a decision. My mother had died of cancer. My stepmother had died of ovarian cancer in her early forties. Was it worth not taking advantage of the possibility of early detection? The drug had terrible side effects, although their progress could be reversed. *Reminiscent of a*

Christa Wolf story I once wrote about, "Self-Experiment: Appendix to a Report," was about a female scientist who chooses to test a drug that will turn her into a man (so she can better understand the man she loves), knowing that there is another drug to reverse the process. The point of course is that after she lives as a man for a while she opts for the second drug. But why? Drugs with severe side effects were sure to affect me more severely. And besides, how quickly would the cyst have to shrink and how far, before one decided whether it was having an effect? And would surgery then be necessary after all?

I consulted friends, colleagues, physicians. My gynecologist refused to offer an opinion, willing to take questions but unwilling to provide me with any kind of answer. Some said I should get a second medical opinion. Others tried to help me decipher which way I was leaning. Others said, "If it were me, I would want to know for sure." *Post-op I learned that there was less than a one percent chance of ovarian cancer, in which case my life expectancy already would have been greatly diminished.*

I opted for surgery.

Surgery was an unknown and ovarian cancer was a ghastly specter. The "chocolate" cysts were identified as "complex," which made them less decipherable. I was convinced that most likely it was endometriosis. But in that case it was better to know exactly where it was and what it looked like. *Hadn't I been reminded often enough that "I had so much in me that I needed to get out," intellectually, in terms of artistic expression, as someone known for her reserve?*

I realize now, in retrospect, that the fear of cancer affected my decision much less than it influenced the advice of others. Having watched my mother die brought it into the realm of experience, and thus made it imaginable. What seemed unimaginable was the thought of taking a drug that would additionally compromise a body without finally being able to recognize that body as ill. Taking a drug would keep me in a work life marked by burnout and immune deficiencies. Choosing surgery would allow me to opt out. Opt out completely, at least temporarily. The day of the surgery, I had no physical symptoms. The most likely prognosis, said the intern two days before *(but then what did she know, she said, having only been at this for five years)* was that they would pluck the cysts off the ovaries and leave everything else intact.

Instead, the surgeon found Stage IV endometriosis. "It was as though someone had poured chocolate syrup all over your abdomen." *"Chocolate": my one vice, my one concession to my (Swiss) nationalist pride.* She spent three hours removing the cysts, which had attached themselves to the bowel and urinary tract, cauterizing the endometrial tissue that had migrated all over my abdominal area. She removed the ovaries and the uterus. "I wouldn't have done you a favor by leaving anything in there." When I came out of anesthesia I was told that I had lost my reproductive organs. She could have sewn me up and consulted me, she said. Could she have prepared me better psychologically in that we never talked about the severest case of a benign condition, only about the possibility of malignancy? she wondered, months later. She hoped that she had been able to remove all of the ovarian tissue. If not it might lead to future pain, which would need to be corrected with more surgery. But a blood test at a later date would indicate whether the estrogen level had dropped sufficiently. That was the last thing she mentioned before I left the hospital—more surgery. I couldn't even imagine it.

Does one mourn the loss of organs?

Would the vagaries of menopause replace those of menstruation?

Am I menopausal, postmenopausal, and do I remember ever having permimenopausal symptoms?

"Surgical" menopause necessarily entails an experience of loss, at the very least, of any one of several reproductive organs. A radical hysterectomy is not castration in as much as it does not involve the removal of an organ principal to sexual pleasure, i.e., the clitoris; it is not amputation in as much as the lost body part is not visible, like a breast. With the loss of these organs comes the loss of the menstrual cycle and a reproductive capacity, all factors constitutive of a gendered capacity, even as a female gender identity is not reducible to them. All women will lose the potential for participation in a reproductive function regardless of whether that potential has ever been realized or not. In as much as femininity should not be confused with maternity, what does it mean to lose, rather than outlive, this potential? What does it mean if one chose not to have children in the first place?

For those who anticipate the removal of their organs, a hysterectomy entails not just loss and subsequent grieving, but also the fear of loss, the fear of losing a capacity for sexual pleasure: what effect will the removal of the uterus, of the cervix, have on the capacity for sexual pleasure? How might estrogen depletion affect a woman's desire, already compromised in myriad ways, for sexual activity? From a medical point of view, any physiological dysfunction induced by menopause can be regulated by replacing the hormones, since for the medical profession there is nothing "natural" about menopause in the first place. On the one hand it doesn't appear "in nature," since in all other species the female reproduces until she dies. On the other hand it is a relatively recent phenomenon in human history, an occurrence, among such large numbers of women, of only this century.

What distinguishes the process of mourning associated with "surgical" menopause from other forms of grieving is the fact of the body's participation. Abdominal surgery is known to require the longest recovery period of any surgery—a year to a year and a half. Recovery entails not just recovering from surgical intervention but readjustment within an entire endocrine system, especially if accompanied by estrogen deprivation. *In my own case HRT was deferred for three months, inducing hot flashes, nights sweats, sleeplessness.* The body can no longer be invoked as an ally against loss because the body itself embodies fragility. The body does not necessarily shift from ally to enemy but induces a different understanding of the dependency between mind and body than the one enabled by and recognizable from youth. It is no longer strong, reliable, pliable, something that can be pushed in order to stabilize emotional volatility. Strategies for pain management developed over a lifetime become useless. *My own surgery has been followed by chronic lower back pain that has greatly curtailed certain activities.* A fatigue is known to set in following hysterectomies that is qualitatively different from any previously experienced, and often not outlived. *In my experience it takes the form of intense sensory overload requiring a form of rest attainable only through physical withdrawal.* Mourning involves not just grieving the lost object, as in a miscarriage, nor a lost opportunity or unrealizable potential, as in infertility. The body itself is both the cause of grief, as body part, and its primary participant, as uncontrollable affect or "moodiness," often diagnosed as depression.

But menopause is not just an effect "precipitated" by surgery; it is also a developmental stage. Natural menopause spans an average of seven years. Much maligned in terms of what it does to women, it is often ignored in terms of what it does for women. What does it mean to have entered that stage in the operating room? To have it coincide with the recovery from major surgery? To experience it only as hormonal deficiency? To recover and in the process to know that one will not be back where one started? And to not know where that might be?

Am I assuming that you don't know any of this?

A story that so intensely involves the body cannot be remembered in the same way. It becomes barely memorable. And yet the entrance into middle age brings with it the promise of memory work that begins with when this was not so, when the body could still be depended on, when healing involved only a body part, when recovery did not imply the permanent transition from one life stage to another. Memory at midlife is about remembering, for the first time, as an adult the experiences one had as an adult. It is about one's own life history becoming memorable and therefore narratable. And thus about a different relationship to history.

Most stories about menopause barely mention hysterectomies. Most stories about hysterectomies assume the presence of a supportive partner, inevitably male. Most feminists assume that every hysterectomy is unnecessary and could or should be avoided.

At the time, I was still mourning the loss of a partner.
I consider myself a feminist.
I identify as queer.

Am I telling too much?
Have I already told all?

For the daughter to mourn the mother means to confront the loss of the one identificatory object that enables a woman to enter culture by mimicking the same-sex model available to men. But to enter culture through the mother must not be confused with entering culture as a mother, especially in the relationship to the mother of a daughter who knew from an early age that she desired neither marriage nor children. Thus the loss of one's reproductive organs does not describe the loss of the maternal function but the mourning of a body image in the form of "another woman."

To mourn, one more time.
To re-member differently.

Chapter 2

Letter to My Mother

Whenever someone mentions menopause, someone else mentions her mother. The mother standing over the stove, tears dripping into the pot. The mother who uses her hand as a fan at the onset of another hot flash. The mother who has been taking estrogen for over thirty years, since the hysterectomy, and still refuses to retire as real estate agent. The mother who had every reproductive organ removed, except for one ovary, which recently has been diagnosed as cancerous.

To hear menopause mentioned is to be reminded of the mother's menopausal symptoms, to remind oneself to ask her what, if anything, she remembers. Because to arrive at menopause is not something one imagines for oneself. It means becoming like the mother, after one has spent years negotiating a separation. It means gradually replacing the mother, often experienced as betrayal.

Most mother/daughter stories are written from the daughter's point of view. This one is no exception.

Dear mother:

Your remoteness is of another magnitude.

I remember when you went through menopause: waking up at 4 a.m., crying; turning red with heat and covered in sweat, which you found most disconcerting in front of a classroom *(and who can blame you, having finally found your way into another profession, a "displaced homemaker," first through immigration, then because of nepotism rules)*. Having finally become the

Samnaun, Switzerland

director of a division at a two-year liberal arts college in the Midwest, and then this, although this turned out to be easy, compared to all the rest. Displaced even further, when we moved for the last time, to California. *What am I doing, living so far from Europe? you would ask yourself.* The job you might have had, had the department chair not given it to his mistress. The job you weren't sure you wanted to have, because your son was living in Switzerland, and, at sixteen, too young to be without his mother. *So he could evade the draft, should it come to that, by renouncing his U.S. citizenship and becoming the Swiss he—and I—were always meant to be.*

I would find you sitting with the curtains still drawn, reading, before the fog had rolled away from that side of the bay, ready to reveal the persimmon tree whose orange fruit hung like holiday ornaments when the branches had shed their leaves. I often found you in tears. Was it menopause? Was it depression? Was it "empty-nest syndrome"? Was it the impending divorce precipitated by more "marital infidelity"? *"Empty-nest syndrome," "marital infidelity" sound so old-fashioned to me. I find myself in tears. All I could do was identify with the mother whose menopause was eclipsing my own college years.* You often called it "senile bed-flight," an expression borrowed from the Swiss-German to describe the fact that as one grew older one needed less sleep. But you were too young for that.

Perhaps it was simply sleep deprivation. That's what they call it now, what used to be called "involutional melancholia" and sent menopausal women to mental institutions in the nineteenth century.

Dear mother:

It sounds so remote.

I never called you that, not even in my letters. Now there is no other way to recall you, since the language I write in is not my mother('s)-tongue. The one you taught me is of no use to the writer (except in children's books and advertisements). For a Swiss, writing means learning to write in German, the language of the foreigner, those who remain other because they are too much the same and those who stigmatize the Swiss for producing inferior forms of writing. How I disliked learning to read and write German, neither of which I was taught in school. The thank-you notes you insisted I send after Christmas, making me wish the holiday would never come. First dictating them to me, then as I grew older, making me compose them myself. I remember writing at the vanity table in your bedroom while you were getting ready to go out. You always asked for my opinion. I was the only honest one, you said. Watching the transformation in your appearance, as the room became increasingly scented by your perfume, was so much more compelling to me than anything I could have expressed in words: the clichés I had to resort to year after year, the abysmal spelling that didn't improve until I was forced to take notes in German at the university, the lack of any real affection for those relatives who lived so far away and never came to visit. By this time a high school English teacher was already telling me I would never be able to write because I had grown up bilingually. In college my prose was still being exposed for its undesirable Germanisms. I come across postcards, marking a page in a book, that you sent from your vacations, leaving us with Babu, our "Russian" grandmother, who was then living in the Italian-speaking part of Switzerland. They are always written in English. The language of voyage, of distance, of the difference between immigrant and offspring.

It's been fifteen years since I last heard your voice, not something one can remember. Half of our age difference. In fifteen years I will have lived as long as you did. After all these years, you still inhabit my dreams. For years afterward I would wake up in the middle of the night, enraged. Now I run into you by chance in my hometown and wonder why you didn't tell me you were coming, afraid to ask. *What language do you dream in? they ask me.*

Disappointment has replaced rage.

How appropriate, for the transition into middle age.

At any rate, you weren't there when it happened to me. Where would you have been, anyway? Would you still be calling me from a public phone booth in "Anywhere, USA" to let me know that you were alive, so as not to let me know that an "extramarital affair" (the settlement agreement had already been drawn up) had taken you to Texas with an engineer from Yugoslavia whose ex-wife painted eyeballs in Berkeley? How discreet of you. Or would it have given us more time, the chance to step out of a mother/daughter script predicated on daughters abandoning their mothers when they leave home, having already been abandoned by the mother (or is it the father) to the "second sex?" The daughter: the most fully realized image of inferiorized femininity, I recently read somewhere.

The only time you ever came to visit me was the spring I spent in Lausanne. Like me, you had been sent to the Vaud in your teens to learn French. You stayed in a hotel and we met for meals on a restaurant terrace, the waves lapping gently against the shore. Just you and me. I had fallen in love for the first time and had already been abandoned for the other woman, the one who could claim the status of fiancée. *How was it possible to love two women at the same time, he kept asking himself, or was he asking me?* You felt so helpless, knowing you couldn't ease my pain. You didn't try. Instead you provided me with the illusion of having what I had always wanted, you, all to myself, without my brother, whom you were convinced needed you more, without my father, whom you needed in ways I could never understand. There, on the shores of the lake of Geneva, surrounded by a language neither of us could claim as our own, we momentarily inhabited a piece of each other's past.

By the time I was receiving those Hollywoodlike phone calls *(maybe it was your lifelong penchant for thrillers)*, time was already running out. Upper back pain had replaced a lifetime of lower back pain. This one, I thought, won't remain a benign, if chronic, condition.

Menopause, reactivating the unfinished business of mourning. *Shouldn't one have finished mourning the mother by now?* Of course I am supposed to mourn the lack of my own motherhood, the children I never had, the "femininity" I was about to lose. But instead I mourned your loss all over again.

But is this what you want to hear?

It's not easy, writing to the dead.

Even if I know I can find you in an Alpine cemetery marked by a weathered wooden cross, flanked on either side by hang-gliders who died in their early thirties. You died young, but you didn't die of youth's recklessness. You asked to have your ashes strewn *(which seemed appropriate for someone who had once taught a course on "Home and Uprootedness in a Technological*

Society") but your son wanted to give you a resting place he could return to. So we drove the grey cardboard box with a string wrapped around it (as they used to do with cakes in old-fashioned German bakeries) to the outskirts of a ski resort in the Alps known as "the city in the mountains." The larches, which burst into flame each fall, keep you company. *As well as the man you always loved and almost married, who recently joined you in a spot not too far away. The charismatic lawyer, his darkly tinted glasses making him look both exotic and slightly menacing. The flirtations you kept up all those years, making your respective spouses look even less desirable. You said you picked the man you thought would make a better father.*

Menopause is not about death; it is about mortality. No one has ever died from it, and yet I can't remember the time, if there was one, between the moment you finished menopause and the time you started dying. Thinking about menopause connects it in some way to death—my own death—having less time to go, most likely, than I have already been given. You were given so little time. A shadow on the lung made them think you had contracted TB from the library in a former TB sanatorium whose doors you opened after years of being locked. Did they really think the bacteria still lurked between the pages of some book or had they simply read too much Thomas Mann? When penicillin proved ineffective, they thought you were losing your mind. The divorce, they thought. Another hysterical woman. No somatic causes. By the time you descended the "magic mountain" for a doctor in the city, it had already metastasized. You lived another month. They never found the primary tumor. One doctor thought you had become hysterical, saying you were afraid of dying *(that didn't sound at all like you; if anything, you seemed too eager)*.

In reality, your lungs were filling up with fluid. The diagnosis of a terminal disease finally made it possible for you to let go. *Would you agree?* Of the two final wishes you had, a trip to Italy and a tour of Zürich, there was only time for the second *(which your son so kindly catered to).* I remember the evening you decided to leave us, when the pain became so great that to alleviate it would mean losing consciousness. It was the day I decided to visit a friend in Basel and by the time the train had brought me back, it was as though the decision had never required my presence in the first place. And the day you died. After taking the tram to the hospital every day for a month, I decided to skip that afternoon. You couldn't recognize me anymore anyway and when the nurses decreased the morphine dosage to increase the possibility of recognition, you sounded like a drunk. That was the day they called. It was a Monday—a Monday in June.

Yours was not the first corpse I had ever seen. When Aunt Alice's heart failed and I saw her still lying in bed with a book in her hand and her glasses on her nose, I thought: This is the serenity I strive for. I realized then that it is only possible in death. The stasis that I equate with perfection I had confused with the end of life. *The books she read were always in French. The daughter of a small-town grocer, her first position was as a governess in a French chateau. She maintained her aristocratic yearnings by having all her clothes made from French cloth (partly necessitated by her excessive weight), by naming their poodle Le Vent, and by taking vacations in Provence, where my uncle transposed the sun-soaked landscapes onto canvases. She repeatedly encouraged him to charge more for his dental work. Instead he hired her without pay to keep the books and made her make due with the "household money" he gave her every month. With the money she was able to save, she continued to indulge in her Francophilic fantasies.*

It was the same month I spent taking my exams for a *license* in literature at the university. I remember shocking one professor because I failed to remember the dates of World War II and misguiding another when I responded with silence to a question about the ending of *Madame Bovary.* Not knowing whether to say that I couldn't remember, or that I hadn't reread the book, or that my mother was dying, I said nothing at all, which he interpreted as meaning: "You're absolutely right; there is no answer," Well, I passed, you'll be happy to know. An old friend of yours accompanied me to graduation, which I insisted on attending in my black skirt, black tights, black clogs, and white socks. Not exactly appropriate attire for a formal occasion, from the Swiss point of view. She said good-bye to me at a tram stop and I walked home, alone, in the foggy night, down the street that connected the university to our family residence. *The one that you left your share of to my brother and me. The other half had also always been destined for the two of us. But just before he died your brother disinherited me and left it all to my brother. He felt property could not be entrusted to an unmarried woman, my father told me, much later. Your son made no effort to offer any restitution (he even gave your jewelry to my sister-in-law), since obviously he was in on it, you might be sorry to hear. Forcing me to sell my share to him. So there it stands, in a fresh coat of pink paint, renovated into rental units, while its owner has moved up the lake to Zürich's wealthiest suburb.* My final farewell to Switzerland. After that there are only brief and sporadic visits. The wooden cross, each time, becomes more weathered.

Menopause reminds us of our mothers, and yet you could never have prepared me for this. It takes all of us by surprise, each time: the irregular periods, the first hot flash, the tears shed too easily, the sleep that comes so lightly. One has no idea when it will happen, how it will happen, for how long. Once it's over, it's as though it was barely worth remembering.

Of course mine happened so differently.

There are ways in which I could never be you: the gregariousness, the charisma, the "blond vamp." *You insisted that deep down you were just as shy, but not like the shyness I inherited from my father.* And there are ways in which I don't have to fear becoming you: the foreign accent, the unhappy marriage, the truncated career.

Yet I remain the immigrant's daughter.

Coming home late at night, sitting at the kitchen table, under the harsh light, amid the dormant appliances, we talk. There was no interest we didn't share, no topic we left untouched. *Only once did I make you reach your limit, when I talked you into taking me to Chicago to see* Gone With the Wind. *I convinced you it would never come to the outskirts. By the time the movie let out it was already dark and you regretted having come, because the garage attendants were all black and, being a Sunday, we were the only white people in the business district. That was the only time you ever showed your fear.* We engaged in endless conversation. You taught me that nothing resisted interpretation. You shared with me an intellectual curiosity coupled with emotional intensity. Which has made it hard—very hard. *The one interest we didn't share was a need for men. Is that the difference that has made all the difference?* I have met only one person with whom I have come close to approximating what you and I had— a woman I fell in love with and shared a house with for six years. Even when she left we knew we would remain best friends. But it is mostly with men that I continue to have the same kinds of conversations—where I learn as much as I do from reading books. Intimate friendships that I used to think had to culminate in sexual intimacy. Now I tell them I'm a lesbian and they don't fall in love with me anymore. Or the men are mostly gay.

It was from you that I learned about gender inequality as not just something one noticed but something one could write about. What you lived as an unbearable contradiction, the one that eventually destroyed you, became my life's work. *I dedicated my first book to you, the one everyone remembers for its unconventional form because the content remains so elusive and people ask whether I chose Woolf and Wolf because they have the same name.* You had first editions of the early "second wave" classics, Simone de Beauvoir, Betty Friedan, some of which you reviewed in your days as a journalist, sending the articles back across the ocean to let the

Swiss know what it was like to "be in America." Along with articles on race. And suburbs. It was you who introduced me to Christa Wolf. *The Quest for Christa T.* has always been your story, even before you became ill, even if the heroine who dies of leukemia did so in her early thirties. The structures of loss and memory have become mine.

Of course by doing it differently I assumed I was doing it better. I was convinced that having a son prevented you from ever fully collaborating with your sex. *Those many nights making lunches. You making my brother's, I making my own. You said it was because I wanted it done my way. But why didn't you require him to make his own, since you found it so oppressive? But there I was again, standing at the kitchen counter, more interested in spending time with you than insisting on how completely unfair it all seemed. That would come later.*

What was it like to be one of three women studying law in Zürich in the 1940s? *Even if also a pioneer, I have always enjoyed the comfort of a cohort, the strength that comes from numbers.* You studied law for quite different political reasons. The war prevented you from leaving the country as a simultaneous interpreter, which was the original plan, so you spent a year, alone, in Geneva, to acquire the diploma. When you first met my father, at the art club that allowed students from both the university and the technical university to visit artists' studios, the first thing you told each other was that you would never get married: you would travel the world as an interpreter and he would go to Latin America to build bridges. Instead you were offered a job as an attorney in a juvenile court, the first woman he had ever recommended for such a position, the professor said. *What would it have been like to practice law not having the vote, denied to women in Switzerland until the year I turned twenty?* Instead you married, emigrated, and looked for a job as a German translator in one of those many Manhattan high-rises, a dime a dozen in those days, after the war. Compared to all those other German-speakers who had flocked to New York, primarily German Jews, your English was abysmal, you said. You never knew how you convinced anyone to give you a job. And then there wasn't enough work, which left you a participant-observer in the world of clerical workers during lunch hour. The eroticized culture of postwar consumerism that would have seemed so foreign to someone with thrift and a sense of an object's longevity instilled in them, as you would have had, as a Swiss. A world of just women that you repeatedly returned to, somehow indifferent to class differences.

The daughter of a feminist who was trained to practice law and ended up teaching foreign languages. *English was the only one of the many languages you spoke where one could detect an accent. The one you never wanted to learn. In those days one could still choose between English and Italian as a third language in the* Gymnasium. *You never had any interest in Anglo-Saxon culture: the steel-grey skies, the pale skin, the male homosociality. So I never made it to Bloomsbury or the Lake District until long after they hired me in an English Department.* The legal system was the one language that couldn't be translated. Besides you were almost thirty and wanted children, you said. In spite of the admiration, if not adoration, expressed in the many condolence letters, you insisted that in the end all that mattered were the two (considered too few in the 1950s and thus unpatriotic) children you bore.

I have never had children. Now I never will. Certainly not without ovaries and a uterus. *Of course these days, that should hardly be a deterrent.* Being a grandmother was one ambition you never had. You even discouraged me from contemplating marriage. *Should I ever contemplate such a thing, let it never be with a Swiss, you once said with utter urgency. You, after all, had married a foreigner. Otherwise the gene pool would continue to degenerate. My brother, you will be happy to know, has once again renewed it by marrying a Norwegian. Only Norwegian is spoken at home. Just to make sure someone maintains the family tradition that never lets anyone feel too certain about their national origins.*

I have never wanted children. For as long as I can remember that is the way it has been. Who knows how it is that one comes to know such things, how it is that one arrives at such certainty *A certainty I associate with the knowledge a transgendered person has about belonging to the opposite sex.* On the one hand I have always resisted normativity, what you understood as a kind of arrogance. *Haven't I often wished for the comfort of conformity, marriage, children, standing at a bus-stop with everyone else on the way to a nine-to-five job?* On the other hand I have always been impatient with "family life," the many hours spent unproductively, in the reproduction of affective ties, resulting in either unbearable boredom or intolerable conflict. Besides, our family has never overindulged in reproduction: your brother had no children; my father has no siblings. *My only cousin is the offspring of a German soldier and a French aristocrat who was adopted after the war by my aging great-uncle and his wife (his former wife's seamstress) who in generation would be my father's cousin and in age has become mine. Their child is my godson, with whom I can only speak French.* Maybe it had already been decided for me, that I was the one who was going to break this pattern of strong women wasting their talents: my grandmother the child prodigy pianist, you the trained attorney, both exiled and unemployed. Having nurtured a mother, who would expect me to do the same for my own children? *The years you spent confiding in me about how unhappy you were in the States, in the suburbs, in your marriage. Disgusted by his infidelity, his silences, his underwear.* I have spent so many years disengaging solitude from self-interestedness, that I would be reluctant to share it again so unconditionally. Only Carolyn Steedman's notion of the "refusal to mother" (which in *Landscape for a Good Woman* does not mean not having children, but having them in order to exchange them for a better way of life that only a husband can provide) has captured an unwillingness on the part of a woman to reproduce herself. In a conversation she and I once had over lunch in a Middleeastern restaurant in a midwestern university town she insisted on having us think about the fact that for the first time in history women didn't have to mother, and what did that mean, precisely, in world-historical terms?

I once thought that by the age of thirty I would have decided, one way or the other. Thirty came and went and I met a woman I committed myself to in a conversation about having a child together. But we never did and even she seems to have changed her mind, although her partner is now the one advocating for motherhood. (In the meantime they've adopted a dog and three cats and the partner has given birth to a son.) Another lover kept insisting on a child she would bear (and I would raise?) as a way of talking herself into a commitment she was never able to make, either to me or a child. That's when I thought I would pop the question to a psychic, to close the chapter. And she did. She confirmed what I had always known, that there were other items on life's plate, but that one had been left in the kitchen.

After the surgeon discovered endometriosis I asked her about infertility. *What made you do that? someone asked.* She responded that it was not a question of whether I would have been infertile, but whether any infertility treatments could have made me fertile. She said there was probably less than a ten percent chance.

Did learning that make a difference? That what I had always imagined to be a choice might have been the outcome not of certainty but of necessity? Not wanting children made me always not-like-a-femme. *I'm not bold and taciturn enough to be a butch. My voice is too soft. My hands are too small. I look good in dresses, even if I feel like I'm in drag.* Aging masculinizes. Two old people in a couple remind me of Chinese revolutionaries in their blue workers' uniforms. Gender differences have disappeared. The sexes return to where they were before puberty. If it is all about attraction for the sake of reproduction, what about the desire not to reproduce? It took me years to attach not wanting children to wanting to be with a woman. Maybe I needed men to show me how to be independent——independent of men——the one thing you couldn't teach me. But that was not something you and I ever talked about. I became involved with women only after your death. Once you were gone I could finally find my way into the hearts and bodies, not just the minds, of other women.

Don't go.

Not yet.

I haven't finished telling you things.

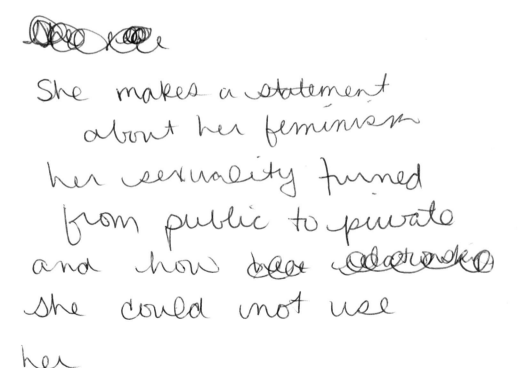

She makes a statement
about her feminism
her sexuality turned
from public to private
and how ~~her~~ ~~elaborate~~
she could not use

her

Chapter 3

Letter to an (Ex-) Lover

What fresh hell is this?

Dorothy Parker

By the time I entered the hospital, we had already ceased being lovers. Intimacy had become the battleground on which we whetted our respective wills. Yet there you were, at the end of each day for three weeks, willing to drive those eight miles so I wouldn't have to spend nights alone. You never took me in your arms again, even when I asked you to, weeks later when I started reading about waning libido and vaginal dryness. Of course I never expected you to accompany me into menopause. You were much too young for that. You continued to talk about moving in together and having a child, even as you wondered, although never enough to want to know, what it would be like to make love to someone who no longer had a cervix.

In the meantime I am seeing someone I have known for twenty years, someone willing to eroticize my scar, who doesn't mind that I no longer have a womb. Something I have never told you. When we were lovers fifteen years ago we planned to live together but I called and asked him not to come. We have remained friends, this man I have been with who most reminds me of a woman. I once told him that and he took it as a compliment. Every couple of months we spend a weekend together, like a clandestine affair. But what is it that we are being unfaithful to? The "confirmed bachelor" and the hysterectomized woman. A different kind of "queer" couple.

It was never clear from the beginning to what extent we attempted or were expected to function as a couple. (Medicalization requires the presence of another, as addressee, as caretaker, as attorney. Someone to mediate between one's body and the medical profession.) At first I went alone on doctor's visits and reported back, but this arrangement made you only more impatient. In true social scientific fashion you wanted the numbers that would predict probabilities. You wanted to retrieve facts from the information superhighway, tracking down articles in obscure medical journals. You wanted quantifiable knowledge to ensure an unknown future. I, on the other hand, wanted to rely on intuition (how feminine of me), collecting the elements that would eventually cohere into a cohesive narrative explaining why this course of action felt like the right one. The one time you agreed to accompany me was the only time I was made to wait for hours. Instead of cherishing them for the stolen moments they provided us in the waiting room (reminiscent of the garden in Thomas More's *Utopia* where time becomes a form of theft enabling the telling of a tale about an ideal society), you insisted on marching up to the counter every few minutes to find out why it was taking so long, making it impossible for us to have a conversation.

In the hospital you were far from the only one to visit me. Every day a different set of people would appear, some of whom had to negotiate interactions with each other, especially on those days when it was difficult for me to stay awake. *I remember when a distinguished poet came and held court from one of the visitor's chairs. I had just started eating after five days of being prohibited the intake even of liquids. I had just finished my first meal and couldn't stand the thought of sitting anymore as a member of the audience. So I made an excuse about having to use the bathroom. That was the moment I accomplished my first noncatherized urination, the one that would allow me to go home. It seemed such a strange juxtaposition, between the words of the accomplished poet, the bodily accomplishment of a convalescent.* One friend thought that you should have been more aggressive about taking on the role of "traffic cop," directing visitor traffic by answering phone calls (which I refused to do) and receiving visitors on a preplanned schedule. But I preferred the randomness, the unpredictability of those who came, the spectacle of people speaking to each other who had arrived for some other purpose, for whom my immobility provided the occasion. And besides, wasn't our whole relationship, after the first few months, about learning how to spend less time together, about forging new ties? *One couple returned too late, a few hours after I had been discharged. They thought I had either died or been wheeled once more into the operating room.* All the bodily processes that needed to be in order returned in a single day. Even the doctor thought I would be spending the weekend. By that time it had been almost a week.

It didn't seem like a long time. I spent most of it dozing, attentive to distant sounds, aware of the women in the room next door. The first one dying of cancer, the second one suffering from gallstones, mostly on a long-distance line to Turkey in a language I couldn't understand. The interruptions of the nurses checking my vital signs seemed somehow comforting. Their styles so different, between the gentleness of the gay male nursing student and the authority of the night nurse from China. I disliked the nurse who woke me up every morning and insisted that I rise from the bed as though I hadn't just had abdominal surgery. She seemed to show no empathy, somehow conveying that even in my condition I had it better than she did, a black woman. The intern who came on the last day to remove my staples had clearly not found his calling. A PhD student in epidemiology, he thought he needed an MD to do the research he wanted. We talked about pain, about whether this procedure would be painful. He didn't know from personal experience and from what most people told him, it wasn't painful, which didn't mean I would experience it that way, he said.

Do you remember the phrase you kept repeating: "Don't worry; I'll be there for you when you have to go through this"? You were so good about bodily processes, the bowel prep you helped me with the night before the operation, the baths you would assist me with when I still had to keep my stitches dry. The incision that you said would never bother you, even though it took a long time for you to remember to look at it, once I was home. *But of course you never touched it.* Your (step)sister had had surgery for endometriosis not long before and so once again by acquiring all the facts of one case, you would already know about another. But she was younger and they left in one ovary. In two months she was back on the court playing tennis tournaments. It was the emotional terrain that proved much more challenging. The uncertainty of whether we were still together or whether these events prolonged a process that should have ended sooner. When an old friend from college flew in from the west coast, she mentioned not wanting to displace you, not wanting to usurp your role. But what was your role? Most people wished that somehow you had played it better.

Your loyalty, and yet your unreliability.

Once I started spending nights on the daybed, before I was able to climb stairs again, you occupied the second floor, where for weeks I wouldn't be able to venture. I think you preferred having your own bed. It was like living in separate apartments in the same house. You would rush home, sometimes quite late, just to be there, losing more and more sleep as the strain of an insufficiently organized worklife and this nightly ritual began to take its toll. Eventually you fell ill—some sort of flu. These nights were your only obligation. And in the end why were they yours, since we hadn't been lovers for months? Because they clearly weren't anyone else's. Of course there were other invitations, to move into a spare bedroom, to have someone come stay for a week. But they never seemed inviting enough and, with you there, I didn't feel obligated to accept them.

I made sure that during the day there would always be someone else to keep me company. And this time I did keep a schedule, on little slips of white paper (where I also kept track of when I took my last pain medication) marking the weekly line-up, making sure someone appeared every day, often to bring a meal and eat it with me. *My ex and her partner brought dinner one evening and wanted to just deposit it and come back for the dishes after I had finished. Not wanting to intrude, a Midwestern custom learned from her mother, the partner explained. But I insisted.* Those were the moments I was able to share that involved not an obsolete sense of obligation but an unanticipated opportunity. Not rushing home ready to collapse but stealing in out of the stream of life, for that expendable tea and sympathy. Spending time in the middle of the afternoon in the middle of the week seemed so sinful, even with the legitimation provided by someone's recovery. Realizing and regretting the fact that in midlife such moments had become so rare. If they had ever been legitimate, but surely, at some point, they had?

But that is not where you were, in the middle of anything. *You had never even set foot in the midwest before.* You had just arrived as an assistant professor. As acting director of the Women's Studies program that year I felt an obligation to welcome the new faculty. *Which I did over lunch in that fern bar. Your shoulder draped over the back of the chair, the collar of your shirt open, under the grey vest you were like James Dean without the cigarette. The authority with which you sent the sandwich back to the kitchen. Not only were you a vegetarian, but you also didn't eat other foods, like mayonnaise. The whif of rakishness that filtered into an all-female enclave that prided itself on sensitivity, cooperation, consensus. You shared the politics—as though someone had frozen a 1970s feminist embryo and let it loose ten years later—but not the politically correct politeness.* You wanted to create a connection, which, in your case, meant staging a seduction. I remember it took almost half a bottle of port for you to get up the courage. Sunday afternoon in the park ended with an embrace and you disappeared off my front porch like a frightened deer. What had I done? I asked myself. *Only later did I understand that you always had to make the first move.* I fell head over heels in love. Or so one thinks. Maybe it was just a fantasy about how sex (at least it wasn't love) could overcome such obvious and utter incompatibility. Maybe I thought being in love would numb me against an administrative job that I had agreed to take out of curiosity and had already begun to resent.

I will be the first to admit that after six years of "marriage" those were the skills (what others did I have?) that I brought to our relationship. They were clearly not the right ones, or so you thought. *In the meantime it is you who have bought a house and settled down with another woman, a garden, and a cat.* That fateful trip to New York that almost proved fatal. *Flying on Christmas Day to a city of Jews, as you put it, was such a treat for this queer gentile.* I had forgotten my journal, which meant buying a writing pad from a newspaper stand which I took to a late-night cafe in Astor Place (now a Starbuck's) where I sat drinking hot tea next to the drafty window in a last desperate attempt to figure out whether I should take the next flight home. I finally called my ex from that windowless basement where we stayed in a room without a door in your former college roommate's apartment. *"So you want to break up with me," you would inquire on a regular basis, which was inevitably followed by "think about sex together." Later it became, "why are you doing this to me?" when sex no longer functioned as panacea but as provocateur.*

You, of course, will remember it differently. You convinced me to stay. We enjoyed shopping for clothes, so you wouldn't look so "schlubby," you said. At the Frick I looked at the paintings while you sat in the courtyard reading *The New York Times,* waiting for me. On your birthday you spent the evening with your hand on someone else's knee. *Reading the entries that have made their way back between the covers of my journal, it becomes clear it should have ended then. After that everything keeps repeating itself: the conflict, the resolutions, the recurrence. Maybe I was seeking a replacement "marriage." Maybe what I wanted was something so undesirable that it would allow me to disavow everything, including the shock from when she walked out after six years, without warning, without the possibility of a second chance. Maybe I wanted to be convinced that, just like I had always thought, marriage sucked.*

Academic ambition coupled with sexual seductions. Just like my father, I thought. My father repeatedly seduced my mother's girlfriends as a way of showing that others wanted what she didn't seem to need. But unlike him, whose conditioned response was, "I don't know what you're talking about," words were your greatest weapon. *How many times did I find myself explaining that losing an argument would not convince me to feel differently?* You couldn't possibly claim ignorance, not after all the psychoanalysis you've read, not after six years of therapy. The only emotion I ever felt for my father was pity. The pity the femme feels for the butch, the butch who desires the femme because she herself appears not to embody the feminine. But also the attraction, for the woman who has shed all the trappings of femininity and takes on life "like a man." The attraction for the tragic figure. The desire to redeem it.

By the time we went to California you had long overstayed your usual three-month limit in a relationship. "A keeper," one of your friends said. *I had to ask what that meant.* We cruised the freeways in a rented Miata with the top down and baseball caps on our heads, as the wind parched our throats. *We have always done best in moving vehicles. Like the trip to Grand Rapids, ostensibly to visit the furniture museum, but actually to have several hours each way with nothing to do but talk. In those days we still took the time and believed that words could be our ally.* You took me to all of your childhood haunts and introduced me to most of your father's. Once again we made the rounds of your ex's. *The only viable subject position. Seduction. Abandonment. And clearly you're seeking redemption again. Asking me what I thought the day after you insisted on introducing me to your new girlfriend. Twenty-four years old. Straight. A graduate student in your department. What is it you want me to say? Moving to the small town I chose to escape to and now you insist on following me. Promising the overabundance from your garden, in exchange for neighborliness, like borrowing my lawnmower.* I should have known. Those ex's all either allowed you to reminisce about the "good old days" in an all-girl's school or brought you up to date on the politics in your part of the profession. *Why did I keep refusing to read the signs?*

The hot springs in the Mendocino mountains. Dry warmth. The disheveled garden. A communal kitchen. Sulphur baths in tiled tubs. Naked bodies wearing the strand of beads that meant they didn't want to be spoken to, carrying books with empty pages waiting to be written on. We settled into the comfort of our circular cabin, filled with the sounds of wildlife and the scent of redwood. Another romantic moment that was never meant to be. When it wasn't anxiety about tenure or a flu that hung on, something else would come to save you from the threat of physical intimacy.

An allergic reaction.

Sometimes to coffee.

This time (supposedly) to the sulphur.

Virginia City, Nevada. Old mine shafts. Tumbleweed that always seems to know where it's going, and then it doesn't care. The wooden boardwalk. The original saloons now cluttered with video poker games. We found the psychic in a recently renovated Victorian house filled to the brim with Victoriana: lace doilies, old dolls, antique children's books. Before even meeting me she had prepared a chart and detailed notes in flowery script. Surprisingly, she told me about herself: how after five miscarriages and three children and the termination of two marriages, the first in death, the second in divorce, she had left the Bay Area (where she had taught parapsychology and metaphysics at Berkeley), was now celibate and active as a painter. She also assists the police in finding missing bodies. When I asked her about us she expressed confidence in our ability to communicate but said I needed to look out for myself. That I would be the one to end it, if necessary. How prophetic.

A turning point. Not the endometriosis. Not the oophorectomy. Not even menopause. Self-affirming, is how I ended up describing the experience. She doesn't tell anyone anything they don't already know, she says.

> She tends to overtax herself both mentally and physically; finding it very difficult to truly relax and turn off. She must guard against being a workoholic and must not let home affairs overburden her.

She talked into a tape that continued to capture the sounds of caged birds, the clock chiming, a train whistle. She didn't predict the course that events would soon take. Instead she said that by the end of the year I would be winding up three major cycles, reaching a crossroad, needing to unload. A natural teacher. A spiritual teacher. "A person who can light up dark places and bring enlightenment to others." *Reminding me of Virginia Woolf's "she will light a torch in that vast chamber where nobody has yet been," of Mary Carmichael, the fictional novelist, writing about the relationship between Olivia and Chloe in a* Room of One's Own.

Everything on my chart shows its opposite. Boxed in between extremes. A giant balancing act. Only "old souls" visit psychics, she tells me. Those with a strong sense of responsibility to fulfill the things they choose. Those originally miscast as an old person in a young body.

> Imagination, inspiration, and emotion are her truest expressions, in spite of her practical side.

Apart from wanting to know the future of our relationship, the focus is on creativity. I have the makings of an artist, she says. Had I ever made money from my art? *In college my design teacher asked what comparative literature was and wondered why I wasn't majoring in studio art.* Neglecting this aspect makes life heavy, too intense, keeping me off balance. Inventiveness. Innovation. Originality. I need to explore those things I haven't been encouraged in. She mentions my sense of color, manual dexterity, being at heart a poet. *Me, a poet, torn between two languages, between silence and speech, isn't that why I repeatedly return to the visual? The words I hide behind as an academic, the abstract, theoretical concepts that only let in a chosen few.* That my soul's identity is much more tied up with creativity, in spite of analytic abilities, a sense of justice, organizational skills. A tendency not to finish things because I think I should be doing something else. *"Conscientious" appeared every year on my report card, beginning in second grade. And every year I had to ask my mother what it meant.* In spite of my determination, my tenacity. *"A determined little somebody," "Aunt Clarinda" said of me at the age of two, outside a farmhouse near Poughkeepsie.* Finding a place that provides the necessary serenity. *That much I have figured out.* Too much confusion—raising children, living on a coast, disharmony in relationships—will keep me off balance. With three new cycles beginning, two of which would take me to the end of my life (a long life, she assured me), energy has to be focused on myself.

She must not empower others to judge her.

A change of pace, of life. A pause. Was this part of the promise held out by menopause? A strong sense of timing. An ability to visualize. A gift for healing.

Your concerns were obviously very different. You had to figure out how to get tenure in a department that hadn't tenured a woman in over a decade, where the female chair was being sued for sex discrimination. Which you did by saying the psychic predicted you wouldn't remain an academic for long, enabling you to pursue interests in political journalism. *Although she did predict you would get this job. Isn't that why you went to her in the first place?* As soon as you arrived you began applying for jobs at other universities. *Of course they would also provide me with one, you promised, rather naively.* Mourning the loss of a bicoastal existence. You mourned the loss of your days in college, finally realizing that becoming an academic was one of the worst ways in which to recapture them. *There was a part of you that never wanted to grow up, that both admired and resented me for being the grown-up. And a part of me that thought someone else's youth would be able to prolong mine.*

In the end it was doing things together we were best at, not being together. For your last birthday *(which you refused to spend as we had planned, in a hotel in the city, instead inviting me to your place where you proceeded to shower me with gifts)* I gift-wrapped the tampons I would never use again and gave them to you. Then I made a list of the things I was going to miss.

And I remembered eating breakfast and reading the newspaper on a paddleboat in the middle of a lake early on a Sunday morning in summer.

Being together was too often just too hard. As lovers we tried so hard to be friends. As colleagues, you thought we had to be lovers. Maybe that's why as ex-lovers, we will finally simply be colleagues. The roses you used to bring me when I sat in the director's office have dried and are beginning to fade. The hot flashes we used to share to warm you up with have since been eliminated by hormone pills. The Shaker bench you built for me still stands naked, waiting for the coat of paint you once promised.

The girlfriend you presented to me may protect you against a sense of having been left, but there is no protection against loss. *You insisted on staying in my house while I was in Hawaii, feeding the cats, doing your laundry, leaving traces of your telephone calls on my bill. Only to tell me, once I was home again, that you were now involved with someone else.* Not wanting to lose your own youth through someone else's menopause, that I can understand. No one wants to get there prematurely.

Now that your girlfriend has gone, you insist on coming back. Making dinner for me and watching television, a show about a female adolescent, the series with the lowest ratings, of course. When you insisted on bringing her with you, I felt like a middle-aged mother whose adolescent daughter is bringing home another girlfriend, putting her head on your shoulder as you share the couch, when it starts to get late. Where am I in all of this?

I've never wanted to be the mother.

I'm not ready to feel that middle-aged.

I don't even like to cook.

This time you can't argue with me, knowing you will win.

This is my one chance to have the final word.

Chapter 4

Letter to a College Friend

The most creative force in the world is the post-menopausal woman with zest.

Margaret Mead

When you mentioned that you would come and stay with me after I came out of the hospital, I felt so fortunate. Few people I knew, not connected by kinship, did such things for each other. But after twenty years of spending Christmas together, and never failing to call each other on our respective birthdays in December, have we not become like blood relations? And now that we have both lost our mothers, we know that this is all there is. This being there for each other. When your mother died and you gave me a set of miniature Mexican dishes that bring good luck in the kitchen, I hung them on a strand by the window. Now whenever we enter each other's houses, we recognize a piece of our own. A different sort of "tradition." You came, your mother explained to her friends, because I had no one to care for me, no family. *Did she mean no mother? No relatives in North America?*

It was my third year in college. I had been invited to go skiing in the Tetons with a friend whose parents were coming to join us from Australia. Shortly before it was time to leave they called to ask me if I knew where their daughter was. I knew nothing. It turned out that unwilling to encounter her father, she had boarded a Greyhound bus in Canada and had stayed seated until she reached the opposite coast. All by herself. I was both disappointed and astonished. What a daring act of defiance, I thought. With nowhere to go, you suggested that I come spend Christmas in central Washington. Twenty years later, the drive across the Cascades to a town of 950 is marked by increasingly familiar signposts. Although the grade is more gentle, the treeline much higher, and the area still unexploited in terms of winter sports, when the air is clear and the snow has freshly fallen, it reminds me of Switzerland. But that is not how or where we met.

We met, of all places, in Italy, members in a program abroad in Florence and housed in one of those villas on the way to Fiesole. My first choice was England. I hesitated to learn another language just well enough to not be able to read the literature. But every morning after the sun rose and before its heat necessitated closing the shutters, I sat in my room at a table overlooking the city, looking up every word I didn't know in Elio Vittorini's *Conversazione in Sicilia*. Eventually I learned the language well enough that I convinced a young man on a street corner in Rome that I was Italian. In spite of my blond hair. Only in Rome.

We met because neither of us fit into the "Greek" crowd that made up most of the student body: the boys who threw garden furniture into the fountain at night, the girls trying to make it with the boys who had had too many beers. We were more interested in the Italians. That way we could improve our language skills and measure our progress. *How many times did we convince them to buy us an ice cream in exchange for something we promised but never delivered? We once made a list, and counted. Apart from those who proposed marriage there was one whose Florentine patronym prevented him, sadly enough, from ever considering matrimony with a foreigner. Instead he presented me with a collection of Cardarelli poems, still inscribed with what by then had already become the memory of "the happiness of our Italian summer."*

As the most proficient Italian speakers (I because it was close to the French I already knew, you because growing up with a

Mexican father had made you more or less conversant in Spanish) we naturally gravitated toward each other. We were both the daughters of immigrants, of fathers who had left their countries of origin in search of a better job. Your father a fruit picker, mine a professor, we nevertheless shared a relationship to "Americanness" that was askew, not straight. *And yet only in the United States could two such daughters end up in the same university classroom, housed in a Florentine villa. Your mother, a Midwesterner, adopted Mexican culture as her own; my mother, an immigrant, pined away for her homeland. Mexico is a country on the other side of the border, rather than across the ocean. "Mexicanness" is a national identity that is about speaking a different language, about having a different relationship to the state. "Biracial" is not a term I have ever heard you use to describe yourself.* We were often joined by a woman whose Afro made the Italians on the street stop, stare, and want to touch it with their hands. We wondered why she wanted to have her hair straightened, in Italy, of all places. To grow an even fuller Afro, she said. Her hair began falling out. She had to keep her head covered with scarves and wigs. She almost dropped out of college. Eventually she moved to LA, you said.

I will never forget the excursion we took one day after lunch to a hillside village for an anthropology class. Field work, they called it. I had not been feeling well, so all I ate for lunch was tomato soup and a blood orange. The small car with too many passengers wound its way too quickly up and down a narrow country road. Finally I said it had to stop. The tomato soup and the blood orange combined into a brilliant red on the side of the road. You were there with me. You didn't flinch. This woman, I thought, has a destiny mapped out for her: something that will require her to be this steadfast under similarly adverse conditions.

Do you remember the trip we took to Viareggio one weekend, wanting to see the ocean but not having the money to spend on a hotel room? *Another one of those challenges we set for our-*

selves, getting something for nothing as a way of resisting our inscription into a sexual economy where we were expected to pay with currency that we did not consider exchangeable. We could always spend the night in the waiting room of the train station, we assured ourselves. Instead, we were repeatedly harrassed, prohibited from sitting at tables after the cafes had closed, because we were two women, unaccompanied. Until we found seclusion in an empty courtyard, trying to keep warm with our shirts and towels until the day would once again make it permissable for us to resist the protection of an interior. That was when I learned that the coldest hour of the night is between four and five in the morning.

We continued to travel together, taking the boat to Greece, trying to take the train through Yugoslavia (we didn't succeed) back to Switzerland to visit my mother. When I left Italy for the last time, on one of those trains that transports a male migrant labor force from southern Europe to the industrialized north, I met someone who insisted on leaving me with one of his few possessions. He was seventeen, on his way to a job in a record-player factory in Tüttlingen.

No pleasure.

No protection.

No conception, thank god.

He continued to send me postcards, postcards that looked empty because his love would be professed in small print around the edges, leaving the center blank. *I don't think I've ever told you this.* Of course I never wrote back.

Once we returned to school in California, we rarely saw each other. You lived off campus in communal housing; I lived on campus in a co-ed co-op named Kairos. After college you went back to Washington to study medicine; I went back to Switzerland to find out how Swiss I was, which, as you know, turned out to be—not very.

For years, it seemed, I followed you from internship to residency to family practice clinics, across the various landscapes of your home state, through the mazes of medical centers, down corridors to cafeterias where we could find neither time together nor something acceptable to eat. *I never understood how those trained to care for the health of others could so learn to ruin their own.* Eventually we caught up with each other and planned a trip to Mexico: Vera Cruz and Mexico City. The open air market. The giant cockroaches. The bull's testicles we found on the beach. My inevitable sunburn, forcing me to acquire a straw hat I still wear when I work in the garden. You speaking Spanish for me, the Italian I once knew having grown rusty and now not really relevant.

Our last fling.

For my forty-third birthday, the first birthday in ten years I find myself alone, the first in eight I wouldn't be spending with my ex, you send me the correspondence you have been receiving from me for the past twenty years. When I opened the box the first letter I came across was the one I sent telling you that she and I had separated. I sobbed uncontrollably. You started reading them, you wrote; had you continued, you might never have sent them back to me. The next time you come to visit, you plan to read them all the way through. I'm still not sure what made you do it. Was it really just an idea you had that led you to look in the atttic? Was it because I had mentioned that you were one of my addressees? Does reaching middle age mean rereading the letters we once wrote because there is too little time to write new ones—a genre left over from Victorian womanhood or a solitary adolescence? Reading further I was reminded of the trip we had planned for years but never took. The one to Alaska, where you had spent one of your residencies. You even gave me a one-year subscription to *Alaska Magazine. Is that why I became such an avid viewer of* Northern Exposure, *I, who otherwise watch so little television? Maybe it's not just because Maggie, the bush pilot, once offered the possibility of a more ambiguous sexual identification. To the point where I insist on passing through Roslyn, Washington, the ostensible Cicely, Alaska. In search of souvenirs for a teenager back home, I say to your brother. All of the indoor scenes are shot in a warehouse near Seattle, the teenager tells me. And Alaska remains a place on the map I have never seen.*

Then came the wedding invitation, for the middle of December, which occasioned the longest letter I ever wrote you. I was rather taken aback when I encountered it in the box, sheets of pastel grey stationary. Here you had decided on a lifelong commitment to someone who was nothing if not a great guy and I was writing about "the function of marriage as patriarchal institution." *I even quoted a lesbian friend who suggested boycotting the event, something she had done, although not without creating a certain amount of friction.* Clearly I felt a sense of loss, losing you to marriage the way I had already lost you to medicine. For some reason I felt the need to put my feminist theory into practice, always easier in writing than in relationships. But I was also trying to convey what it was that I had learned all those years while you were becoming a doctor—trying to make it more concrete. Least tangible were the signs of the beginning of a "coming-out" process. I write about a sexual identity in limbo, between asexuality and bisexuality, one that could only resolve itself through the expression of same-sex desire. It seemed about as far as one could get from the subject position of the "wife."

Unclear.

Uncertain.

Unrepresentable.

I refer to your marriage as the crossroad in our relationship, even more so than having children—a viewpoint I'm not sure you would share. *Just another example of how letters really belong to the sender, not the addressee. Which would lead one to believe that most correspondences remain in the wrong hands.* When I write of friendship as life's subtext, I am honing my skills as literary critic. When I write of how for most women the most important affective ties are with other women—even as they are expected to choose a man and make him their emotional center—I am practicing my feminism. But I am clearly also seeking a language for my queerness. Another language of loss, this time about the friendship between two women when one of them chooses marriage: the oldest story in the book. The story even in that book that many women still read in search of something that will represent their lesbianism, Radclyffe Hall's *The Well of Loneliness.*

You married an entomologist who willingly followed you back to the town of 950. A family of doctors, including his mother who went to Smith and dropped out of medical school to marry a doctor and a father who has a medical school building named after him. *I remember him finding it strange that even though he was marrying you, I had known you much longer. What did that mean? he wondered.*

Another letter I could not help noticing was one I had typed on parchment paper. It was dated September 28, 1981 and contains a long quote from Virginia Woolf's *Three Guineas*—another attempt at proving to you, and myself, that what I was learning could make the personal political. The quote contains passages such as, "In short, you will have to lead the same lives and profess the same loyalties that professional men have professed for many centuries," *(which is exactly what you were reluctant to do, by threatening to give up your career in order to have children).* And what kind of life is that, Woolf asks herself. "Sight goes. They have no time to look at pictures. Sound goes. They have no time to listen to music. Speech goes. They have no time for conversation. . . . What then remains of a human being who has lost sight, sound, and a sense of proportion? Only a cripple in a cave." Clearly, that was not what I was advocating for.

I continue in my own words: "On the other hand, how will the professions change, if we leave them? Will what a woman writes in forty years from now echo our own plight, as our plight echoes

Virginia Woolf's? One would hope that in nearly a century words will come to describe a different situation. And yet change moves slowly, like a pregnant woman, and only if each of us contributes her share. Like you, who wish not to become like your father, whose work took him away from his family, I wish not to become like my mother, whose family took her away from her work. Nor do I wish to become like my father, but like him, have chosen my work, not at the expense of a family (perhaps each generation has only one lesson it can learn), but without one. I will be no more than a partial parent to the children of my friends." I'm not sure I convinced you. But you established yourself as a family practitioner in a small-town clinic where as the first woman doctor you continually had to set precedents, in writing, for part-time work, for maternity leave. Now you, in turn, attend continuing education courses at the teaching hospital where I live, as your way of staying in touch.

One could tell this story like one of those women's narratives from the early 1970s, "the one marries, the other doesn't." Marge Piercy's *Small Changes* comes to mind. Or the film by Agnes Varda, *One Sings, the Other Doesn't*. But that seems too easy. Like any "family" member, you would like to see me settle down in some kind of permanent partnership. The sex of the other person seeming not to matter. Although the person does. There are few you have really approved of, my ex being the exception. I'm still not sure you understand why it is that she left. I think you're still not sure how it is that I came to know that I was lesbian. I used to think that normativity was something you wanted to impose on others; now I understand it as something you are defending single-handedly. (The only one of four siblings married, with children.) Middle age has meant giving up on the hope of normativity for others. Your brother will never marry; I will never have children. But it was you who introduced me to a particular version of the nonnormative. You were the first woman I ever met for whom being with another woman was not second best to being with a man. I actually say that in one of the letters I wrote you. "The one marries, the other doesn't" is too easy because that's where the story ends, and ours hasn't yet. Besides, lesbianism isn't just an alternative form of closure to the marriage plot.

By the time I called you about my medical conundrum I was seeking both advice from a doctor and reassurance from a friend. You brought to bear years of developing a professional manner. You tried to make me say myself which way I was leaning. You tried to present the point of view of a health care provider, without influencing me in any way. Finally at one point you said: "It's usually better to know what's going on. That way you can figure out how to deal with things from there." *You must have been thinking of your mother, dying of lymphoma, "as though she were slowly being strangled by a snake." The fluid that caused her legs to swell seeping into the abdomen. Twenty years ago she was given two months to live. A recurrence from when you were a child, when you were expected to take over the household, which is what has made you so practical, able to take charge of any household, including mine. Especially mine, that weekend you came to stay.*

By the time I was driven home from the hospital (by a friend who diligently tried to avoid every bump in the road) you had already set up the bed in the dayroom, moving furniture around to try to make it more comfortable for me. You had already made tomato and potato leek soups (without a recipe, of course), filling the freezer with one-person batches. You had already baked a tin of banana muffins, which I could barely eat because everything seemed so dry. Combining ingredients you found with those you bought, you left me with food for weeks to come.

Months later, I was still cutting each apple I ate into thin slices, like the ones you prepared for me. *⎦ Sentiment*

A year later, I'm still making soups, filling the freezer with individual portions. *Months later I had still only regained four of the twelve pounds I had lost.* I still haven't regained my sweet tooth. I've returned to being a strict vegetarian. I drink even less than I used to, which was almost nothing.

You were with me that first night, when I attempted, in vain, to re-create the comfort of the hospital bed. You were there when I called, in the middle of the night, because I was afraid. I was so uncomfortable, disoriented by my new location, adjusting to a different narcotic. Each night I would get up between three and four in the morning and stroll around the house. *I've never been a night person.* But being in motion was by far the most comfortable position. ("Walking is good exercise. Around the block, in a shopping mall, doing light housework," said the "discharge instruction sheet for patients following abdominal surgery.") Eventually I would lie down, in the hope that sleep would find me again. *This was before I was put on HRT. Before I could even think about the meaning of menopause. Before it was confirmed that my estrogen level, as intended, had indeed plummeted. Before I was willing to recognize that what I was having were hot flashes.* "Somedays you will find that you'll feel extremely tired, in which case make sure you rest," the doctor said. ("No more than a quarter of daytime hours should be spent in bed," said that same "discharge instruction sheet.") Over a year later I still find myself having to resort to bed rest at eight o'clock at night at the end of a strenuous week, which I never realize I've had, until I'm so exhausted I can't eat and can barely move.

Because I ended up staying in the hospital longer than anticipated, you had to leave the next day. But during the evening's conversation (where we lost all track of time) you were kind enough to indulge me with answers to my questions about how one becomes able to perform surgeries. You explained how the bowel (in all of its length) is removed during the operation and then replaced into the abdominal cavity. How it is reinstated in a kind of fan shape. And how when this is done toward the end of the operation and the anesthesiologist has begun decreasing the dosage, it tends to lose its flexibility and potentially pops out.

"Boing," you said. That made me laugh, in spite of the pain it produced and which you said I could contain by pressing a pillow against my abdomen. *Some hysterectomized women are convinced that once the intestine has been removed and placed on the operating table, it never feels the same again; it never regains all its functions; it never completely adjusts to a space that has been deprived of its other occupants.*

From menopause we meandered to maternity. (By the time most women reach my age they have at least been in the hospital to give birth.) You talked about how horrendous your second labor was. How the doctors insisted on natural childbirth (because the first one had been a caesarean). Your body has never completely recovered from the damage, you say. How when you had almost finished healing you had to return to the hospital in Seattle to have a gortex patch placed on his heart. Later steroids used to combat a sinus infection seem to have affected the ovaries. Your estrogen level is lower than it should be, you think. Maybe it's time to look into some low-level Premarin, you say. *You're always pulling something out of that briefcase that you don't know you have—donations from a pharmaceutical company.* You certainly encouraged me to take hormones as soon as I could. "It will make you feel so much better."

We talked about the youth of my gynecologist. "She will make a better doctor when she gets older," you said, and I agreed. Still steeped in the bliss of maternity, "my ladies who just gave birth," she calls them, having twice given birth herself in recent years. *An Interflex student here at the university, she finished both college and medical school in six years.* Menopause is something she hears about from her patients—a remote possibility. *"Estrogen solves everything. And without ovaries it's so much easier, because naturally produced hormones aren't interfering with the dosage. And without a uterus, there's no danger of uterine cancer, and therefore no need to add progestin."* Something I had to do anyway for a year, since endometrio-

sis is estrogen dependent. When I asked her about breast cancer, she said, "As an American woman you have a very high chance of getting breast cancer, one in nine." *This made me feel particularly patriotic.* "This way," she added, "you will be more closely monitored."

The next morning my ex drove you to the airport.

For you, this is so much par for the course, a part of your professional life. I'm never sure what you think about the fact that I spend so much time trying to make sense of it—that I would even take the time to write it down. It's not practical, is what I imagine you saying. *Although I've recently heard you say, with some regret, that you've never done an impractical thing in your life.* There are lives to be saved, or at least prolonged. A daughter that needs to be raised. *A daughter even more different from you than I am, refusing to wear jeans because someone might mistake her for a boy, not wanting to go berry-picking because there are too many bugs, choosing a Barbie doll lunchbox. You decide not to say anything.*

Twenty years ago.

Menopause is about saying "twenty years ago" and still being able to refer to experiences one had as an adult.

We talk of traveling together again, once the children are grown, once we've retired. In the meantime, with my books and my pen, with the only things I know of to make meaning out of all this, I will come and stay in the "blockhouse" on the other side of the orchard, by the road.

A place to do your writing, you say.

And at noon you can stop by for lunch.

in writing letters *therapeutic* *daughter* *lesbian* *friend* *lover* *academic* *feminist*

Chapter 5

Letter to My Father

I often gave way to self-pity.
Do I deserve this? I suppose I must.
I wouldn't be here otherwise. Was there
a moment when I actually chose this?
I don't remember, but there could have been.
What's wrong about self-pity, anyway?
With my legs dangling down familiarly
over a crater's edge, I told myself
"Pity should begin at home," So the more
pity I felt, the more I felt at home.

Elizabeth Bishop, "Crusoe in England"

You have always preferred being away to staying at home—whenever possible, without leaving an itinerary. Certainly no forwarding address. The point was not to stay in touch. "Work" has offered a lifetime of alibis, explaining why you were gone; why you didn't speak even when you were here; why we had to leave, every summer; why we moved—every several years, it seemed. "Work" was like a mistress, like a wife. When it took you away it filled my mother with resentment; when it brought you back she resisted readjusting. It was the thing you were married to that enabled endless infidelities. The point was not to keep them a secret. The point was to make them known. Whenever I wanted to cry, my mother said, "Not in front of him. You're giving him what he wants."

These days you dispense much more liberally with the itinerary, willingly reciting a list of names: Cambridge, Moscow, Paris, Palo Alto, Davos (or is it Moscow, Basel, Naples, Cambridge, Washington, DC?). Occasionally you call just before you leave some place you've been for months, putting me in a position of never being able to call back. The first thing you mention is how I'm never home. *Is there some confusion here between filial and conjugal duties?* Then you ask about my physical health (as though that were all paternity required). Then you rattle off the itinerary. (The engineer who has achieved (as mathematician) international notoriety, his desirability outpacing his mobility, especially postretirement, it seems.) Which I neither write down nor remember. Why would I? I could always leave a message on the answering machine in an apartment in a ski resort in the alps, or send a fax. And I'm assuming someone else would do the same.

You've always preferred being someone's guest. *That way you neither have to do the housekeeping nor engage in monetary exchange to have it done. You feel at home for as long as you like and when it's time to leave, no one would expect otherwise.* Which is why whenever you're in the country you invite yourself for Thanksgiving. You could, of course, just leave the country, but when that's not convenient, you give me a call. *Only, of course, when I've become the only woman in the picture again.* Besides, it offers the semblance of some kind of "family." Father-daughter. The relationship that Freud refused to recognize. Repressed, I think, is the word. The father's impotence when confronted with raising a daughter. The daughter's anxiety about becoming a surrogate spouse. Repressed except as seduction scenes, staged even with my so-called stepsisters. So where does that leave me, a surrogate son?

Maybe that's why it's been so difficult to find the words, the right words, any words.

You called to say you were coming before I knew I would be receiving you from the daybed. What a coincidence that you would actually be here for part of my recovery. Certainly not something you could have planned, not with that kind of *Wanderlust. The daybed, a blessing in disguise. Whenever I needed to retreat from the barrage of words, I could always say it was time to rest again. Too soon since the last visit, I hadn't forgotten how the words beat down like bullets.* I would reenter the sun-filled room populous with potted plants. Light filtering through the leaves and patterns dancing on the floor. The study vacated by my ex, it had long remained

uninhabited,

underfurnished,

unfinished.

I was in the process of reclaiming it, knees propped up on pillows, listening to books on tape, talking on the phone, dozing off in the middle of the morning. Convalescence. An existence most like that of a cat: when and where do I lie down? For how long? Somewhere between illness and health. One knows one is healing but one can't remember what it feels like to be well. Afraid one won't recognize it when one gets there. Afraid that getting there will always be approximate. Convalescence is not something one would ever wish for. And yet, once imposed, one wonders why. Why it is that one has spent so much time avoiding what doesn't count as work. How it is that one has come to forget that there are other ways of being. It is not somewhere one can stay. Inhibited in one's mobility, the impulse is to linger, on the way to somewhere else. *Those middle-aged Victorian invalids, paradoxically, figured out that increased mobility—intellectual, political—could be achieved by staying in bed. Elizabeth Barrett Browning. Florence Nightingale. Alice James.* In this transitory state one learns how to feel located again. In one's body, because that is all there is. At home, because one can't go anywhere. The drowsiness. The lethargy. The daydreams. Some days I read only *The New Yorker*, because I have to get away. Some days nothing at all, because I can't even get that far. For a month I couldn't even think about writing in my journal. Much too difficult to contemplate what all of this might mean.

The daybed now long gone, the room has been repossessed again by the plants that my ex abandoned and asked me to adopt, at the very last minute, that morning she moved to western Massachusetts with her girlfriend, three cats and a dog, a motorcycle, and a U-Haul. *When I entered the empty apartment she had shared with her, I thought, what a mistake. How could I have agreed to this? But now the first hibiscus has bloomed, joining the ranks of the other orphaned flora when the Goethe Insitute transferred the local director to Algeria. Algiers, not a place he was able to stay.* Lined up on the table facing the bay window that lets in the evening sun. No computer. No phone. No piles of student papers asking to be read. A place to write something other than letters of recommendation or committee meeting minutes. Strains of music wafting in from another room. At night, I turn the chair toward the fireplace and pick up where I left off, whatever I was reading lying on the trunk my great uncle (also an engineer, never married, his first name Hermann) took with him into the Swiss military. Now it has "J.H." (for Jurik, traces of your Russian origins), "New York, NY" written on the top in indelible white ink, one of the last vestiges of an immigrant past.

Dislocation began with an immigration officer asking whether there had been insanity or syphillis in the family. My mother's middle-class sensibility was insulted, and she told him so. And with a bribe. My mother tried to make you understand that the reason he kept saying, "I'm going to have to open this trunk," was not because he wanted to, but because he wanted something else, which you eventually provided in the form of a ten dollar bill. Postwar. Maids, ministers, and teachers received instant entrance visas.

I'm always reminding my students that complicated names indicate a complicated character. *Villanelle as opposed to Henri. C.S. Lewis as opposed to Joy.* Occasionally one of them will remind me of how utterly patriarchal mine is. Ironic, they will say, for a feminist. "Mr. Man" is its most literal translation. It is your mother's maiden name, but I have yet to meet a relative who spells it the same way. The name you acquired from your father—Ostroumov—you changed because you thought it was too difficult (for whom?). Even for the Swiss. Anya Ostroumoff: the name I might have had, the person I might have been. Instead I became Anneli. Anneli kämpft um Sonne und Freiheit, *the first book I read on my own in German, about a girl who seeks to escape factory life for the out-of-doors.* The Swiss diminutive that prevents anyone (especially those marked by feminine endings) from ever growing up. *Wasn't my mother always Betli?* When finally I insisted that everyone call me Anne *(the Anna from my maternal grandmother on my birth certificate not outliving its traces of foreignness and old ladydom)* my uncle (with his waning short-term memory) would look at me and draw a blank. Growing up made me nameless, at least in a language where I could only be little or old. My one hope was English, where words remain ungendered.

The intrepid world traveler, when you're here, I can't get you to leave the house. And you're only getting worse, more restless when you're gone, more sedentary when you're here. As though the place where I live has so little to offer you might as well consider it a form of rest cure. *The rooms are too cold, the bed is too hard for a shoulder with a degenerative bone condition, you complain.* Once you pulled Virginia Woolf's *A Room of One's Own* off my shelf, read the whole thing in front of the space heater and proceeded to lecture me on it. I, who have spent years in lecture halls, interpreting this text for students. The next time you started reading around in Christa Wolf's collected essays, and I, in my usual inability to remain articulate, asked whether you had brought the volume in your suitcase. Well, so much for knowing the contents of my own library. *Do you remember the obsession you once had for Margeurite Duras? You read all of her novels in French, the last of which my brother and I had to procure by making a special trip into Paris from the airport, the fall we experienced Indian summer together on a bench in Central Park. My last memory of him was tinged with fondness. I was so tired I almost made the café table lose its balance, which he teased me about for weeks. His way of displaying affection—or was it anxiety—was to make my mother and me the butt of endless jokes, with you as his collaborator. You arrived at the breakfast table every morning to deliver the insights from the night before. It nearly drove my mother crazy.*

This time you had just returned from your first visit to "the former Soviet Union," after sixty years. And you won't stop telling me about "the second in command of the Russian Orthodox church" whom you had met, just like that, by going up to his table in the hotel dining room in Zermatt when you heard him speaking Russian with his sister. *"How do you explain someone like that being able to spend several weeks at a time in a Swiss ski resort?" you begin interrogating me. Of course these questions are always posed in such a way that only you can answer them. I, once again, reduced to the blitherings of someone barely born. Of course it doesn't help that we are usually speaking Swiss-German, which gives me a double disadvantage. While I am still searching for vocabulary items, you are already preparing the next sermonette.* Now you've been adopted by this man, this "Patriarch," as he's called in the church hierarchy, intent on bringing you back into the fold. "This is where you belong," he says. "You've been living your whole life in the diaspora" (which one, I wonder). "Doesn't it matter to him that you don't believe in God?" I ask. You answer with that shrug that means it's never crossed your mind before. "Haven't you wanted to go there yourself?" you ask. "You're one-quarter Russian, after all." Still not knowing how Swiss I am, or how American, how could I possibly begin to think about how Russian I am? Russian, the one language I've never learned to speak. Which is why the

Russian side has always provided the narrative of possibility. The professional artists. My grandmother was a child prodigy, playing the piano at the Russian court when she was twelve. My grandfather, originally an attorney, was trained by my grandmother as an opera singer, when the revolution came. He had an affair with the leading lady on a world tour (which took him to America) which he confessed to her upon his return. My grandmother demanded a divorce, immediately, something she regretted the rest of her life. "I left my soul in Russia," she would say to me. She would let me pick an object out of a glass case in her Basel apartment, filled to the brim with things. She even used her oven for storage space. One time I picked a brightly colored teapot with an exotic shape, like an onion. It was too small to be of any use. The only vestige I have from a place I have never seen, a language I've never learned, a life I might have lived.

By the time she brought you back to Switzerland, because of Stalin and the famine, her career was over. *She smuggled you out on a forged passport, almost losing you at the train station, then placed you in a TB sanatorium in the mountains, the same ski resort where my brother finished high school and my mother lies buried in the cemetery. You were only twelve at the time; you spoke not a word of German.* She could have played on the radio. Instead she gave piano lessons. She never played for us. She had two grand pianos on the terrace during the ten years she spent in the Tessin having remarried into an old Basel family. She taught me how to play (the only progress I ever made) but no one has inherited her perfect pitch.

Your mother: when you came home from school with a broken arm, she insisted that you tidy up the bookshelf (which you had failed to do) before she would take you to the doctor. Your father: he took you to the toy store and when you couldn't decide between two sets of dishes, he bought you both.

All of these stories I have learned from my mother. Sometimes I would ask you if they were true. You couldn't remember. You wouldn't elaborate. Occasionally you would remind me of your days in boyhood gangs on Moscow streets, of nights in the Bolshoi theater, always the same seat, for the son of the pianist. An alternative form of child care, even then, surrounded by an aesthetic avant-garde that would become my academic field of interest. *The modernist lithographs—Picasso, Braque, Miro—that my mother collected from a dealer who came over from Paris that year we lived in London and you threatened to leave us for your pregnant secretary. The art deco lamp you brought me all the way from Spain for my fortieth birthday.* Your father continued to write, keeping a journal in the form of letters he addressed to you in Russian, that you were only able to read once you went back again for the first time. On the Swiss side, the artists never give up their professions. A doctor. A dentist. More than Sunday painters, they study with masters and their paintings reside in permanent collections, but they always play it safe. Landscapes. Still lifes. It's the Swissness in all of us. You who became an engineer instead of a filmmaker. I who will, most likely, confine creative activity to the security of sabbaticals.

The only way to get you out of the house is to go on walks, which you agree to, even more than once a day. *Now when I see older women taking brisk strolls through unscenic landscapes or residential areas without sidewalks, I recognize them as engaged in a postmenopausal activity I call "antiosteoporosis exercise."* On one such walk I attempt to broach a different topic of conversation. Something I could possibly get interested in. Something we might have in common. So I ask, "When did you realize that you had entered middle age, or when did middle age end and old age begin for you?" Another one of those it-never-crossed-my-mind shrugs. "Do you want to talk about middle age now or shall I go on with my story?" As always, the question already has an answer. The tears rolling down my face go unnoticed.

Don't cry. That's what he wants.

You show me photographs of the cul-de-sac where you had lived in Moscow, still the site of an historically preserved residence that once belonged to an artist and currently houses his paintings. It is now also the site of a high-rise that has replaced the building you lived in, the one-room apartment with a communal kitchen and bath. You show me pictures of rural landscapes in spring, dotted with wooden houses and wildflowers, which I try to match up with memories of the Russian novels I once devoured. You show me a shot of the Patriarch's bed, where you spent the night, your clothes still strewn on the chair. *What homoerotic fantasy was this fulfilling? I wonder. What scene from the Oedipal narrative? Why this obsession with male authority figures?* When I mention, at some point, that in your endless tales about people I didn't know you focused almost exclusively on social status, you respond with, "What else is there?" And yet behind that ambition you have always preserved an admirable modesty. You never parade your accomplishments, just your acquaintances.

At one point I feel so frustrated that I finally blurted out: "We've known each other for forty years and all you talk about is something that happened to you in the last few months that has nothing to do with me." That stops you in your tracks and makes you humble. It forces you to try to ask me a question or two. Of course it doesn't last long. And then what? Silence. *Which we dreaded more than anything, my brother and I, when my mother would leave for a week, for Mexico, for instance, because her spring break didn't coincide with anyone else's. One year he sprained his thumb and I broke into hives. You spent all evening in the emergency room.*

If my mother had died any sooner,
I would never have learned to speak.

In the end the only thing we have in common is also the most taboo—my mother, your first wife. *You have just divorced your third, who unlike the other two, hasn't died yet, although she, too, is suffering from a terminal illness. When my mother was dying you never crossed the Atlantic to see her, saying it might induce another heart attack, leaving my brother and me to make all the funeral arrangements, to liquidate the apartment, since my uncle, who had just lost his wife, couldn't be counted on. She, of course, unwillingly stayed in the Bay Area when you had your heart attack just as she was, finally, about to leave for the final separation. And then you had the gall to say, after her death, that had she lived you would have gotten back together. A last-ditch effort to have the settlement agreement annulled so that you would inherit everything.*

The father's inability to mourn. For years you refused to mention her name. Knowing you can't you replace her. Knowing you will never be able to take her place.

The ceaseless motion protects you from the fear of arriving somewhere where there is no "there-there."

The wall of words prevents you from having to encounter the silence at the center.

World famous in your field, since retirement you've received enough professional invitations for several lifetimes. But at what expense? My own ambivalence about ambition. Two different models of the academic. It's difficult not to see them as starkly gendered. The oldest daughter who never quite becomes a son—carrying on the family name, surpassing the father's income-producing potential. (What would it mean to be a daughter?) Academia, the only profession where the best work gets done while one is not officially working. The last workplace that offers independence and legitimates creative activity with a guarantee of lifetime security. At least for my generation. Which, I must admit, may be the last.

Thanksgiving dinner was relatively uneventful. Friends came whom you've met several times by now, here and in California, but you insist on not remembering. Apparently I broke "our tradition" by serving meat. *When I first met them, they were on a strict macrobiotic diet. Now I seem to have become the dogmatic vegetarian.* Not knowing if I would have the strength to make enough side dishes, I was forced to rely on take-out, upscale, of course. So I too am losing my memory. *Or was it just a misunderstanding about what had come to be called a "tradition"?*

I continue to be polite. I put breakfast on the table every morning, "light housekeeping," a recommended form of exercise (a spoon, not a knife for the jam; a cup, not a mug, for the tea). And I listen. Or at least I pretend to listen. And every now and then, when I can't hold it in any longer, I blurt it all out.

And wish that my mother had lived, instead.

You phone and ask me why I haven't called. Otherwise you never comment on what it is I should or should not be doing with my life. As long as I have a profession and remain a homeowner, you rest assured and feel you've done your job. You never inquire about children. Once you wondered whether my sexuality had reoriented itself. My lesbianism is something you are curious about, allowing you to ponder your own same-sex desires, which are nonexistent, you conclude. You have always supported me in my intellectual endeavors, not just financially. The year my mother died, you sat down with me on the couch to help me decide about graduate schools. Only once did you suggest that maybe I would be happier teaching at a liberal arts college rather than a research university. You ask me how I'm feeling. You hope I'm getting better. You suggest seeing an acupuncturist for my chronic lower back pain.

What will I do the next time you visit, when I won't be able to retreat into the dayroom? When I can't put on the headphones, close my eyes, disappear into the interior?

When there will be no next time?

Chapter 6

Letter to a Gay Man

When you invited me to Hawaii, for some additional "R and R," as you put it, I paused. I had been south in the winter only two other times in my life, both times encumbered by the effects of overexposure because my fair skin failed to protect me against the instant change in climate made possible by air travel. *I am not one of those people who judges and/or chooses a place by its weather. I have an affinity for the north: its frozen expanses, its scattered inhabitants, its stillness.* But this time I had the time. I had the financial resources. I had the desire (or so I thought) to travel to a place I had never been. I certainly wanted to further the healing. *At times I felt it was all about fulfilling other people's desires, the longing for leisure, for another latitude.* My therapist sensed that this could be more therapeutic than talk. When I came back and still exhibited intense tearfulness, she began to feel disarmed and suggested antidepressants. But I resisted. I knew this wasn't depression. *The sleep deprivation that accompanies menopause is known to resemble jet lag.*

My only constraint was my body. Would I be able to carry even a flight bag across endless stretches of airport corridor? Would I be able to survive the additional sleep disturbances caused by the time change? Would I be feeling better or worse from the hormone therapy treatments commencing just a few days before departure?

I knew you would look after me. You, who have regularly prepared meals with such devotion. Often insisting on sushi,

THE MOANA HOTEL - 1920

Honolulu, Hawaii

which you know is my favorite food. Although I was never invited alone for dinner, once my ex and I separated. *And you would never let yourself be invited back.* You met my ex first, that year she worked as a secretary while you were completing an MFA, having been trained as a lawyer. Having already renounced the practices of one profession, you were preparing for another, working on a PhD for which you could have submitted a novel; instead you became interested in film, dedicated to kung-fu films. Learning about fish hatcheries, but never making it beyond the training camp for the peace corps. Learning Japanese, but never receiving the funding for a journey to Japan. We had never spent more than a few hours together, in the comfort of the apartment you never shared, sparsely furnished, overheated, the poster of a scantily clad male gymnast, clamoring for one's attention.

You suggested that I come during the week your uncle asked you to house-sit. "He has an expensive house with an exquisite view," you said. "With a pool for you to swim in." You knew swimming was my favorite form of exercise. *One night we came home and you turned on the lights for me. Even though it was unseasonably cold, I swam through the illuminated water, under the star-pocked sky. You began playing the piano, on the grand in the next room. It couldn't have been more romantic, and yet romance couldn't have been farther from our minds. I was trying to revive the plots of nineteenth century novels I had read, the adulterous heroines who spend their whole lives in search of scenes like this to share with their lovers. You hadn't played for years, you said. Clearly, you had had a distinguished beginning as a pianist—glories of a lost youth, haunted by having to fulfill the desires of others because one's own could never be expressed.* You didn't tell me that the house contained Chinese antiques, was protected by a $50,000 burglar alarm system, and that your uncle had once accused you of removing a jade figurine that he had simply misplaced.

If not now, when?

On the airplane I counted my hot flashes. This was three days after I had begun hormone replacement therapy. They gently warmed the torso, occasionally producing a bead of sweat along the brow. In as much as I tend to be cold much of the time, they were rarely unpleasant. In as much as they come from nowhere and for no apparent reason, they resemble the uncanny. In as much as they are a constant reminder of middle age, one hopes each time that this one will be the last. They seemed to arrive on an average of every hour.

Hot flashes are thought to occur most frequently between six and nine in the evening; they are thought to last anywhere from an average of thirteen months to as long as it would take to reach the end of natural menopause (for those who have arrived at it surgically) to the rest of one's life. There is no consensus as to whether it is the decreasing amount or the diminished amount of estrogen that is their cause. At night, when they are renamed "night sweats," they prove to be a much less welcomed guest. *(I would sleep only a few hours before I started waking up with increasing frequency. This had been going on since surgery, for almost three months. It was not the sweating that proved most unpleasant, but the chills that followed.)* Although there is no scientific understanding of what causes hot flashes, night sweats did not seem to be the cause of my sleeplessness. A more likely explanation of what I experienced is the following:

> It is theorized that night sweats occur when the adrenals are triggered (usually by a sound) and flood the blood with adrenalin, which causes a hot flash. (Whether by the flash itself, the chill after, or the adrenalin-induced panic preceding, you are awakened.) Producing adrenalin stresses the adrenals, however. Every time this cycle occurs, the adrenals are stressed a little more and thus are more easily triggered by smaller and smaller sounds, resulting in more and more frequent sleep disruptions. (Susun Weed, *Menopausal Years: The Wise Woman War,* pp. 90-91).

Within another day my hot flashes were reduced to one a day. Two months later, they had virtually disappeared, only very occasionally precipitated by a stressful situation or an overheated environment. Now, over a year later, I realize that those hot flashes marked the beginning and end of my menopause. And yet I will never know what was menopause, what was the hysterectomy, what was recovering from surgery.

I will never forget that morning, several days after I arrived, when I had that terrible bout of nausea shortly after breakfast, which I assumed was caused by the hormone pills, since that is one of their known side effects. You were so attentive, telling me to lie down, bringing me a glass of water. You were so concerned, ready to enlist the services of your sister, a pharmacist, and your mother, who worked in a geriatric clinic. I eventually called my doctor's nurse, who seemed to be getting a vicarious thrill from knowing that I was calling from Hawaii. The doctor responded, "Give her the patch," but the nurse overrode her and said I should continue taking the pills, eating something every two hours, avoiding hunger pains at all cost. I tried to eat enough but the discomfort persisted. Eventually I started taking the pills at night.

But why am I telling you this? Can you be interested in my healing, having no acquaintance with, not even an interest in, this kind of body?

You who have a body that can never have this experience, encapsulated in its difference, isolated in its integrity. There is no medical speciality specializing in its vagaries, its pathologies, its fruitfulness.

My body is a scarred body, a thin body, that reminds me more of adolescence than middle age. My skin is almost translucent, reminiscent of my grandmother's; my hair is so short I am mistaken for a man. ("Paper or plastic, sir?" I am asked in the supermarket.) Certainly it would have to be a gay man they are mistaking me for. What then is it that still makes me so certain about the gender I belong to?

For a time, after I came home from the hospital, dressed in flannel pajamas and a man's bathrobe—like a dandy—I read only memoirs by gay men—Monette's *Becoming a Man*, Duberman's *Cures*, Ackerley's *My Father and Myself*. As though the relationship between body, identity, and disease were much more aptly figured there than in *Our Bodies, Ourselves*. Literature on menopause virtually ignores hysterectomies; literature on hysterectomies begins with how most of them are unnecessary (one cartoon, while the patient is being rolled into the operating room by a male doctor, carries the caption: "I hope you can justify this hysterectomy to my women's health group"). It ends with either how one's sex life will be over (without HRT) or with HRT one's life will end shortly through cancer. (The most recent study shows that after five years of use, risk for breast cancer increases thirty to forty percent.) Not the kind of reading material that would offer any form of solace. This is one of those moments where I feel totally let down by something called the "women's community." The personal can't always be politicized. The fight against patriarchy being waged against pharmaceutical firms can't always be waged on the body of the individual woman. For the first time I feel as if I'm sleeping with the enemy. So the life histories of gay men provide the most comforting and provocative rendering of a story that involves negotiating the relationship between sexual activity and a stigmatized sexual identity in relation to a body that increasingly feels not like one's own. Most of these men have neither the support of same-sex communities nor of stable partnerships, which is why they resort to the pen. On the one hand their story will never be mine; on the other hand it's the story of a body that has been produced by medical discourses that nevertheless resists its usurpation. From inversion to perversion to AIDS.

The feminine and gay men: flowers, interiors, opera.

Your relationship to the feminine is not through identity, but identification. Identification, not desire. Desire is located elsewhere. Desire for bodies on the beach, in martial arts magazines, on the video monitor. For bodies perfectly sculpted that mirror your own. Look, but don't touch. Whenever they come too close, should they ever leap off the screen, you will run away. The feminine is easier to get close to.

You greet me at the airport with a lei, now dried, its extraordinary fragrance long gone. Yes, I did manage to carry my bag along the interminable internal runways. On the way back it will seem so much easier. A sign of my continuing recovery.

In preparation, I read a Marxist history of Hawaii. I can't just go as a tourist. I must also go as a student. I read a collection of short stories written by a friend of yours, *Talking to the Dead*.

They take place in Hawaii. They read like prose poems. But what am I looking for? What did I think I will find? I read a series of essays by Maxine Hong Kingston (which you recommended), illustrated with original woodcuts, a limited edition. *Available only in the university's rare book room, where I venture, where I have never been. Oak paneling. Only pencils, no pens. A handful of devotees return, day after day, to a community of scholarly readers. Like a nine-to-five job, the comfort of knowing where to go and what to do. Not knowing what one will find.* I hold the book in my hand. I study the woodcuts, some of which fold out over several pages. I read the prose pieces, all of which seem too short, like Italian ices that end just as one is beginning to savor the taste. Maybe I would just rather return to this room. Maybe this is all I need or want to learn about where I am going.

No one has told me about the double rainbows, the "liquid sunshine," that absconding with lava rock from Kilauea will leave one cursed.

I have no idea that here all of my house plants live outdoors and that the annuals I painstakingly plant every year (only to repeat the gesture the next) reach the size of bushes and require regular pruning. You told me that you began growing orchids in elementary school. *"There are nearly twenty-thousand species of orchids—it is the largest flowering-plant family on earth. . . . To desire orchids is to have a desire that can never be fully requited. A collector who wants one of every orchid species will die before even coming close"* (Susan Orlean, "Orchid Fever," *The New Yorker,* January 23, 1995, p. 42). One member of your family has been visiting the grave of your brother every day for three years, with flowers, the watering can permanently housed in the trunk of the car. You will finish relandscaping your mother's garden and then you will leave.

Leave the island. What I initially thought would be a sense of confinement on such a small land mass becomes an ever-present sense of limitless ocean on every side.

From your uncle's house we look down on the hotel where Bill, Hillary, and Chelsea spend a vacation, only to find themselves on the front page of a newspaper cavorting in the pool next to an image of a woman slogging her way through Midwest floodwaters. Their behavior was considered in poor taste, they were advised to leave early.

I swim in a lagoon you take me to just a stone's throw from Waikiki, but ever so empty, so quiet. Like a large pool with salt water, without waves. Here I regain confidence in my body, exposing it to the sun, immersing it in the water, buoyed by the salt that attaches itself to the hairs on my skin, and eventually turns them a lighter shade of pale. Initially you accompany me, although you say you don't like to swim. Even as you tell me stories from a past where you regularly swam with others. Eventually you just drop me off at the park's edge. *In the end, I am never quite sure whether you have invited me for the company I would provide, or simply to render me a service in my sorry state.*

Our days revolve around the needs of the dog and your mother's work schedule. A "min pin" (miniature pincer), you chose it because it combined unfriendliness with intelligence (is this your elusive ideal?) It never warms up to me. Snapping at my heels whenever I move from room to room, as though we had never met. You, on the other hand, speak to it in a language of love, if not desire. The intonation of your voice accommodates itself to the exigencies of intimacy reserved for a lover. *Did you know that Ackerley has written a book titled* My Dog Tulip, *to whom he dedicates his other works?* At times the words become indecipherable; they sound foreign. I ask whether you are speaking Japanese, the language you have learned from your mother, but you say no.

Clearly the family has been reconfigured in such a way that you and your mother function as conjugal couple with the dog as third term in the triangle. Your father, long since retired from the military, provides a retiring presence, not speaking, not spoken to. Your sister, who has found an alternative "family" in the community of the church, appears for dinner several evenings a week. But she too remains unable to penetrate the privacy of the language, both spoken and unspoken, that you share with your mother. The mother of a son who doesn't want to know that he is gay but who knows that he will never leave her for another woman. What he does with men—lust after them, sleep with them—is nothing that would jeopardize his relationship to her.

Every afternoon you pick up your mother with the dog in the car. Every day she greets the dog by repeating over and over again, "Oh you're so cute." Having completed at least preliminary preparations, you and she make dinner together *(you can't stand the fact that your father doesn't work, doesn't help, and so you put yourself in his supposedly proper place, by identifying not with him, but with the subordination of the wife)* and continue the conversation characteristic of a companionate marriage. By the last evening your mother refers to me in the third person. Now I know that I too have joined the ranks of the redundant.

An hour later it is time to take the dog for a walk, before it gets dark. Due to recurring kidney stones, the dog needs to be walked at least two hours every day, a dictum you, unlike your mother, faithfully adhere to. I join you because I too am recovering, not from something that might recur but from something that encourages me to stay in motion. This is my favorite time of day. The brisk walk through the military base. *Diminished only by the visit we have to pay each time we arrive at the two abandoned kittens, demanded by the dog. Left there when they barely had their eyes open, unsheltered from the sun, the public provides for them by supplying food in plastic bowls that still have their price stickers. They look shocked. I never see them play together. In my own fragile state, their sight brings tears to my eyes, the result of some misplaced overidentification. In your last letter you say they and all of their paraphenalia have disappeared—a private adoption, you presume. Or an untimely end.* The breeze picks up from the ocean as the sun sets behind the palm trees. The generals' houses are strung around a circle like beads: screened-in verandas, monkey trees casting their lacelike leaves against the sky, lights turned on but the shades not yet drawn, revealing the family heirlooms meant to give an air of permanency to a life marked by regular upheaval.

The briskness of the walk is not conducive to conversation. You insist on keeping up with the dog, but no one, including your mother, can keep up with you. Occasionally, when I agree to conform to the dog's pace, I ask you a question, about life in the military, the horticulture of indigenous plants, the cultural origins of the island, as a way to make conversation. You always provide informative answers. You are always polite. When I can't keep up, I don't let the resentment at feeling less valued than the dog fill the space of my loneliness. I imagine what it would be like to live in one of those houses. Of course I always imagine myself the officer, never his wife.

Later I wonder whether you want me to ask about your dissertation, or initiate a discussion about sumo wrestling as a form of cross-dressing. I am not a member of your dissertation committee, which is one way of preserving a friendship. But I am also not ready to be a mentor. I am still so tired. I have so much healing to do. I have to care for myself, finally. I suggest things you might read. I send you one of the books you felt you couldn't afford at the bookstore. Did I hold up my end of the bargain?

I sometimes think not.

As the days wear on and we do less and less together (have I overstayed my welcome?), but you are willing to chauffeur me anywhere I want to go (as long as it isn't during rush hour), you suggest that I have tea at the Moana. Built in 1901, which makes it the oldest hotel on Waikiki, it displays vestiges of its former past on the second floor, offering historical tours every morning at eleven. *From the display cases I learn that those who traveled by steamer are expected to throw their leis overboard on their return trip so they can wash up on shore, signifying an eventual return to Hawaii.* There I sit on the Banyan Veranda (named after the enormous tree in the center of the courtyard) in a high-back wicker chair surrounded by Japanese tourists (mostly women), sipping English tea, eating finger sandwiches, reading *Women of the 14th Moon: Writings on Menopause.* As soon as I sit down, a fan is placed, most unexpectedly, on my place-setting, accompanied by a card with the following inscription:

> During a visit to Waikiki in 1923, Spanish novelist V. Blasco Ibanez was relaxing in the garden of the Moana Hotel when he noted an aroma which stood out from the scent of the tropical flowers around him. He asked one of his companions about the distinctive fragrance, only to learn that it came from the hotel's wooden panels which were made of pure sandalwood from island groves.

> To rekindle some of that old Moana magic, we have placed a sandalwood fan on your table to use while you are with us on The Banyan Veranda.

The book that I am reading has on its cover a reproduction of "Hot Flash Fan," a series of panels created in collaboration by fifty-two women artists. What an unlikely coincidence, I am thinking. Some kind of sign.

The hot flash displaced by tropical heat.

The fan a simulacrum of a tropical breeze.

The climate of the climacteric.

Sandalwood no longer grows in Hawai; it has all been harvested. The fan, no doubt, was made in Southeast Asia, then shipped back for commercial purposes, which now means tourist trinkets. The sunlight dances on the water. Surfers ride the distant waves. Strains of Polynesian music mingle with the seabreeze.

As a native you shun this tourist scene, in search of a different destination: Las Vegas. I had read about the Hawaiian "diaspora" in my Marxist history—young people who resist the tourist economy by refusing to work for the hotel industry. But what did Las Vegas have to offer that was any different? An oasis in the desert instead of a tropical island; the artificiality of an interminable day as opposed to an endless summer. A city that doesn't pretend to be anything other than what it is, rather than an island that has been exploited to make it something it can no longer be. It makes Hawaii seem old-fashioned. You defend this regular destination by pointing out how close one is to the Sierras (i.e., nature), how good the food is (in spite of being served to thousands), how inexpensive three days and two nights are (given Hawaii's distance from the mainland). I have never been to Las Vegas. I have no real desire to go.

Hawaii is as far east as I have ever traveled, given my Eurocentric origins. The tourism of highly developed resorts (swimming, golf, tennis, the location barely matters) makes the self-designed, if well-worn paths of the European traveler seem hopelessly outdated. If in Europe there is too much to see (masterpieces, markets, monuments), here, there is nothing to do. And yet part of the attraction is that what one can do is always the same: the amenities provided for, the activities predictable. Each resort competes because it is newer, has more recreational opportunities, offers greater insularity. There is no desire for stimulation—just relaxation—in a climate that is meteorologically safe.

When I returned to the Midwestern winter of record cold and snowfall (Lake Superior froze over for the first time in sixteen years), I continued to take walks, alone, outdoors. I ended up, by chance, at the Conservatory. Hot and humid, an artificial place that takes one to another climate without the need for travel plans. There I see, again, for the first time, all the plants I had never seen before I arrived in Hawaii: the sausage tree, birds of paradise. *And having recently read a book on travel literature, I am made to realize that conservatories, such as the Field Museum (of natural history), are the products of a similar imperialistic imagination.*

You say you will bring back the bottle of French dessert wine I brought but that we never drank, on your next visit to the mainland.

Thank you for the wonderful time.

Chapter 7

Letter to (Two) Young Women

According to the Civil Service Retirement System, the average female retiree lives to the age of 85, and retires at age 60. Maybe there's too much emphasis on the years prior to 40.

Madeline Mullen

Both of you were scholar-athletes, players on the field hockey team. I should have known, at the time, that you knew each other. One of you an English major, the other appearing in one of my Women's Studies classes. *The worst course I have ever taught, "Autobiography and Ethnicity." Autobiography, where I thought the undisciplined could meet on interdisciplinary territory. The only course I have ever completely given up on. First the lesbians alienated the straight women and they failed to return after the first day of class. Then most of those remaining either had been or currently were involved with each other. Finally those who identified as lesbian but did not seek entrance into their cabal, otherwise known as "community," were severely ostracized as not the right kind of dyke. Communication took place under rather than above table, making it impossible for me to read the signs. Finally I gave up and said, "We'll do whatever you want." They chose small-group discussions. By that point it didn't matter what it was they were discussing. Maybe it was autobiographical.* All of this I learned only as you filled me in much later and informed me of your own (mal)treatment as defector.

Negotiating the hazardous terrain of the English paper, you were never quite certain how to position yourself between the theoretical and the personal, or whether it might just be easier to memorize the muscles in an athletic medicine textbook. *When writing anything becomes too difficult, I suggest writing it in the form of a letter, to a friend, an educated lay person, even one's mother, if it comes to that. Advice I seem to have taken myself, on occasion. On more than one, as you've reminded me, when you mentioned the parentheticals I use in the chapter I write as an epistle in my first book.* Somehow you imagine that by writing a letter to me about my book, a part of which I once wrote in letter form, you will be able to recover a relationship that has really only come into being through letter-writing. That you will be able to chart a course in the student-teacher relationship, as a student working on a masters degree in rhetoric, as a teacher who sends her letters from a "writing center," where you wonder what it is, exactly, that you are teaching. You compliment me as a teacher, "finding ways to address these issues in highly political and subversive while at the same time informative and insightful ways is how I often recollect your teaching." You encourage me in my administrative capacities. "Chuckled in that it is you who have been in the wings and groomed for the position. And yes, it is you who have invested the time and the energy in the program. With that comes yet another responsibility in your already busy schedule. But also the recognition . . . not that that may be high on your priority list, but the visibility is important for younger women to see. As you know." You always remember the person. You are already aware of the costs. *How little I knew about such things when I was your age.*

You began to write to me as soon as you moved to Seattle, knowing that sooner or later I would appear for a visit. My relationship to you began with a serious crush, something I have never mentioned, except to my ex, while we were still living together. The only other student I have fallen in love with, in all these years. She asked me what I wanted to do. I tried hard to imagine what it was I wanted. All I could think of was inviting you to our house so we could garden together. Gardening was the one thing my ex didn't insist on doing together. At times I resented the responsibility. *I'm not a passionate gardener. But I like living outside, so gardening becomes a form of outdoor interior decorating.* I'm not sure she understood. Was that all, she asked? That was all I could think of, I answered. There was nothing to be (un)done.

Your letters are filled with advice. Now I'm no longer the role model. Now I am being told what to do. At least we agreed about the need for surgery. After that it's all about keeping me informed, about Neuro-Emotional Technique (NET), Sacral Occipital Technique (SOT), and applied kiniesiology. Holistic approaches to healing. I take that back, you did at one point write that I was one of the few people in North America actively engaged in my own healing.

I take your advice. I see an acupuncturist.

I return to my chiropractor, even after she says that the surgery and hormonal changes have made my body almost unrecognizable, the tensions so deep that her adjustments can't really reach them. I visit several massage therapists, each time because someone else tells me theirs has performed miracles. Each time I realize it is not the massage, but the relationship with the therapist that has been building up over years. One is too rough, another too anxious. I finally return to a young gay male friend who was a former costume designer, but who is now trying to build up a practice. A month-long stay in the hospital, more surgery, steps away from death's door (all of which his partner, a dancer, has set to movement and performed on stage) he has decided to devote himself to the healing of others.

I know you don't approve. He's not the person you recommended. But I remain engaged in my own healing.

When I arrive at their house, the evening sun is filtering through blue and green bottles of every shape and size lined up against the front window; all the cards with red are displayed frontally in the postcard rack; an old desk is receiving a fresh coat of bright green paint. "It's a bit too bright," he says, comparing it wistfully to the swatch. The next time I come it stands opposite a dark pink wall lined with dozens of madonnas in miniature frames. The candles, the medieval chant music, the scent of sandalwood.

Together, from very different bodies, years apart in age, we exchange notes on how to manage the chronic lower back pain that continues to plague us since our respective surgeries. We have both had organs removed. His was the colon, a vital organ whose function can be regulated through pharmaceuticals; mine, a nonvital organ that creates havoc with the endocrine system when not regulated by pharmaceuticals. He has studied with a wise-woman, and has become a polarity therapist. He recommends herbal teas and tinctures. He tells me the breaststroke I swim twice a week for fifty lengths could be stressful to the lower back. I describe my daily half-hour sequence of exercises. If the sit-ups are too painful, maybe I should think about doing those at night. He recommends a video he follows three days a week to strengthen the abs, some bodybuilder, to drool over or swear at, depending on the day. We exchange our favorite yoga poses, supine twists and sitting poses with a strap. I tell him about sleeping on his side with a pillow between his legs, a recommendation from my yoga teacher. He tells me that when he becomes too sleep deprived (from the pain), it helps to go to bed early. His doctor has told him that sleep between 8 p.m. and midnight provides the deepest rest—something I've always known, but only recently have had to act on with any regularity. Every few weeks I crave ten to twelve hours of bed rest, just lying there, allowing the entire body to relax. Otherwise I lose my appetite. Otherwise I feel like I'm just dragging my body around, like a little red wagon on a string that is too thin. Otherwise I'm too tired even to sleep. This, in addition to swimming, the sauna, as additional forms of relaxation.

When you ask about my healing, you never just ask about my back. Your questions are much more philosophical: "What does the body do with the surgical removal of organs that form/inform its history?" Where did you learn to ask questions like that? *Is this something one can teach?* Why are you the only one who has wondered whether my mourning has been for my own physical loss or the loss of important women in my life? *Is this a question only a lesbian would ask?* Maybe one has to be young to understand middle age. Maybe one has to be young to be philosophical about menopause. The language you use to describe your own body is that of circuitry, blockages, and the freeing of pathways. *The body began on the hockey field until no fewer than nine gynecologists failed to diagnose your pain as endometriosis; until a back injury, during one of your last games, sent you to a chiropractor (forbidden while you were still officially an athlete), who discovered a sprain in your fifth lumbar; which you traced to a weight-lifting injury (some football coach adding a fifty-pound weight too many) that caused you to tear several ligaments; that damaged the nerves, you now think, sending signals to the uterus that failed to regulate the blood supply that formed into adhesions that the body read as infection that compromised your immune system.* But your language also insists that the body has a memory, that organs are the sites of emotion and that practices such as applied kinesiology can change a body's history and thus promote healing. The body that was once trained as an athlete you wanted to turn into a firefighter, but it looks as if your back won't let you. Instead, you follow, vicariously, your friend Rachel, who is close to curling the necessary eighty-five pounds, placed third out of two hundred in a mile and a half run, the first in her heat, running against almost all men.

You completely understand when I start spinning out my own version of a midlife crisis, my fantasy about taking an institutional leave to learn acupuncture. The fantasy that has always run parallel to my academic career, that of a private practice. The independence and the individual interaction. Working five or six hours a day, the rest devoted to artistic activity. *Like my massage therapist, who each time I come shows me the books he has made, currently on consignment at a local gallery, vintage photographs he's found, on their covers.* Never having to speak to more than one person at a time. How is it that I ever thought I could reach fifty people at once? And all of them strangers? Until fourteen weeks later their faces have all become familiar, only to never be seen again. I even sent away for literature from a psychoanalytic institute in New York. When I was in graduate school, when jobs were scarce, when tenure was uncertain. But I never seriously had to consider another option. Until now. Only now I would like to learn about the body. A whole new body of knowledge. Without a body not in pain, that becomes all there is. Listening to the person speak about his or her body, then to the body itself. All I have worked with are minds. Together we work and rework something into existence neither of us knew could be made to exist. Only in language. Listening to them speak about their writing, listening to their writing as it tries to speak. I'm better as a tutor than as a teacher. *So much talk. I feel so visually deprived.* You send me the address, the telephone number of the acupuncture school. Now it is you who are studying math, before going to work, in order to eventually attend chiropractor school. *Now it is I who will be living vicariously through you.*

You are less interested in the body, and more in the stories it forces one to tell. How they change with age. You still seek advice, as though as former teacher, I somehow had the answer: "How does one mentally discipline oneself?" "How do you shut your mind off long enough to rest?" Coaching, you say, teaches one how to act confident and convincing, even if no one ends up happy. Valuable preparation for teaching, you suggest. You've found a place, at least temporarily, where you can do both, at a prep school for girls. *Brownstone gothic is a welcomed alternative to the bed of a truck, you mention in more than one*

private at public

agency   juxtaposing

letter. There you attempt to "negotiate honesty with a blanket of self-restraining privacy" as teacher/friend/authority figure/dorm parent. Something you have always negotiated with great finesse. What is it, exactly, that you want to protect? Inscribing yourself in the stories of others: your mother, the coaches who have become your friends, now, your pupils. Your own story still untold. Except as a Division I athlete, encouraged to apply for an international field hockey officiating rating. What will become of the athlete's body, joints older than they should be, a prime candidate for osteoporosis, you wonder.

But it is not your body that holds your interest. Just as it is not your own reticence you wish to overcome. You listen carefully to those who unexpectedly let go of their reserve. These women, now twice your age, who begin to talk to you of aging, of loss. It comes as a shock, "the sense of reflectiveness, the tangible awareness of change and passage of time." You hear them "contradicting in emotional intensity that which I have heard from these women before." You wonder why. You notice the stark simplicity of their metaphors: "Now when I go to the doctor I get a bit uneasy. It's like I'm a car in for the 45,000 mile checkup. Major things start breaking down. And it's more expensive to fix." You wonder about women who have had no children being at higher risk for endometriosis. About the connection between endometriosis and hysterectomies. Your fasci~tion, you say, has to do with imagining the future. A future   we can never know or be prepared for. But know   ll take the sting out of the ordeal, "thus leav emotions."

What happens to the emotions in r their reticence? Do they become m middle-aged friends suggests that v resign ourselves. That we overcom ful fallacy. And learn to forgive. O duality

A model of maturity rather than one of relived adolescence. Best captured by the recently cancelled TV show, *My So-Called Life*. The best of television, it had the lowest ratings. Even an Internet campaign couldn't keep it on the air. Its protagonist was an adolescent girl, against the backdrop of her baby-boom parents. Adolescence and middle age were parallel plots. Similar longings, doubts, indecisions, only this time accompanied by memories. Supposedly one had no idea what one was doing then. Again one is taken by surprise. This time because one was told that once would be enough. Again, I'm cross- and misidentifying. I identify with the woman entering early middle age, her negotiation of responsibilities, her renegotiations of her past; but I'm not married, I'm not a parent. I identify with the adolescent girl. The one I once was but never saw represented? The one I have become again, beyond rather than facing the potential for reproduction? *I watch every episode. I save the last one on tape. I almost never watch television. I'm hooked. This, the popular cultural representation of my recovery, not the PBS specials on menopause, which I find completely alienating. I'm not in a couple. I don't have intercourse.* If I could remember what it was like to be in high school, maybe I could understand the early years of college. If I could remember adolescence, maybe I could begin to understand middle age. And that way we could both keep speaking across the gap of generations. That is my other fantasy. I remain an academic, but I begin to pursue nonacademic writing. Writing once more an aesthetic practice informed by memory rather than reading.

The alternative to teaching/coaching in a prep school would be the opportunity to work on a cultural studies project. "Sports as a piece of culture." "The gendering of bodies on athletic fields." Should I be encouraging you? Will you ask me to recommend for a PhD? I've met another young woman interested in omies, much more interested than her own mother, who ne, and said there was nothing to say. She began by working with a nurse who became interested in its fictional representations, as a way to think about the experience of her patients. Three novels, a handful of short stories, a smattering of poems. I recommend Nathan Shaham's *The Rosendorf Quartet* and Wendy Wasserstein's *The Sisters Rosenzweig* for her senior essay. The first about four musicians, German Jews, who emigrate to Palestine in the 1930s; the second about three sisters, American Jews, who meet in London for the oldest sister's birthday. In each case the hysterectomy (the result of an ovarian abscess; of incest and a botched abortion), a seemingly trivial piece of information, becomes crucial to the plot. In each case it serves to explain the only woman character or the oldest female character as a successful professional (viola player, international banker), someone who "acts like a man." Either "ready to close shop" or sexually promiscuous. "Hard" is the recurring attribute. Attractive to men, attracted to men. The "straight lesbian." *I'm slightly envious. I would like to be writing this essay. But without the student's need for a topic, I never would have been able to go back to these texts at all.*

When you first wrote to ask how I was doing, I told you.

On November 8 *(the day the bridge at Mostar fell to the Serbs, the bridge a colleague and I had crossed just a few years before in pursuit of a noonday meal after attending a conference in Dubrovnik)* I entered the hospital for pelvic surgery. Pelvic surgery requires the longest recovery time of any surgery, up to a year. It can lead to depression two to three years later. According to the discharge literature, postoperative recovery has been completed in six to eight weeks when it is once again safe to lift heavy things: children, pets, groceries.

On October 11 I had an ultrasound. *I immediately recognized the medical technician in that dreary hospital basement as "family": the gait weighted downward, the lack of sentiment, the technological expertise. The career in the military she had recently abandoned gave it away, if nothing else. She asked me whether I wanted to introduce the penile projection into my vagina myself or whether she should do it. I had trouble figuring out the right answer. Since she wasn't allowed to interpret any of the results for me, the last thing she did was wish me luck.*

Is this what you want to hear?

You who have only reached the age of twenty-four. *Women your age are worried about getting pregnant, or trying not to. Women my age are trying to get pregnant, or coming to terms with infertility.*

I remember you mentioning that your mother had a hysterectomy and was advised against estrogen because of cysts she once had removed from her breast. But she never talked to you about menopause. That you knew two coaches under the age of forty who both have had radical hysterectomies, and talk of taking care of their bodies rather than taking them for granted. That you've been "adopted" into a circle of middle-aged lesbians who talk about such things.

So you already know much more than I did.

The books I've read on hysterectomies are almost all about why and how not to have one. (As a colleague recently put it: "Feminists don't have hysterectomies.") But what about those of us for whom it is already too late? They can only make one feel like another statistic in the medical establishment's plot to reap profits from unnecessary surgery and subsequent drug sales. Only one book I've read considers a hysterectomy justifiable in the case of endometriosis: "If endometriosis is so extensive and has invaded so many organs that it cannot be adequately treated with laser surgery and if hormone therapy proves unsuccessful, then hysterectomy must be considered" (Martin Greenberg, *Hysterectomy,* Chapter 4). It makes me feel first like a victim and then like a collaborator. To "politicize" menopause has meant not seeing it as a hormone deficiency disease but as a developmental stage. But for those of us who have undergone surgical menopause it often means being out of developmental sync, entering midlife prematurely. What does seem subversive is that I'm telling you all this, that I've decided to devote my research leave to writing it down. As you've said yourself, writing is, after all, part of what one does in this profession.

When I finally arrive in Seattle, I bring a friend along. You instantly position yourselves as rivals. He says not a word; you do all the talking. I try to pretend there is nothing to notice, in an attempt to mediate. From your letter waiting for me when I get back, I realize not that you wished I had come alone, but that what I had done was bring back, embodied, a piece of your past.

"What does the body do with the removal of organs that form/inform its history?"

Chapter 8

[handwritten: c duality/level/experience/identity]

Letter to My (God) Mother

	calcium
1 c milk	330 mg
1 c yogurt	300 mg
1 oz cheese	250 mg
1 c cottage cheese	200 mg
3 ½ oz. sardines	250 mg
1 c broccoli	140 mg
1 c black beans	270 mg
4 oz tofu 150	150 mg

After my mother died, there you were.

After all those years.

Godmother, "a woman sponsor for a child in baptism," we are told. You and she met in the Swiss military, of all places, during the war. The equivalent of the WACS. After the war, she asked you to be my godmother. The cultural mother to a baby boomer. Eventually, to a motherless daughter.

The baptism: June 22, 1952. Wasserkirche, Zürich. A mere six months old. My first trip to Switzerland. My first passport. Not much to distinguish me from other infants. It was the same church my parents were married in, a small romanesque building perched on stilts about the river Limmat where they perform chamber music in the evenings and leave the door open for visitors during the day. There I've returned, again and again, to its architectural simplicity, to its entangled memories.

That was, apparently, the only time you ever met my god-father. You ask about him, periodically. He has never left Zürich. He still lives in his parents' house. He still resides in the town on the side of the lake with the Lindt chocolate factory, where Thomas Mann lived, where my grandmother died, in a sanatorium. That's what they called it. It was really (according to my mother) a retirement home for white-collar criminals and a resting place for old people. He has spent his days in the university library (to conserve heating oil at home) where he has been writing a book on World War II for most of his life (for which he has read everything ever written on the subject in a major European language). After he caught TB in the military, he did not complete his PhD (in political economy) until he reached his forties, and never held a regular job. *There I find him, year after year, in the reading room. We leave for the nearest café, where he imparts to me his infinite knowledge about things of limited interest to me. I try to steer him in the direction of Gottfried Keller or European unification, about which he can be equally eloquent. I'm not always successful. We keep returning to the front.* Eventually he writes a bi-weekly column, photograph and all, for the Swiss equivalent of *The Wall Street Journal*. He never marries, although he has been engaged twice and he still hasn't finished his book. He still wears the same white shirts, the collars yellowing. He looks ageless, in spite of his grey hair, now almost white. I have never seen him without a coat and tie.

I am his godchild, but I am also his last link to my mother. They were students at the university together. I'm certain he was in love with her, but she was never interested in more than his friendship. He has held this against her, even as his devotion to her as a friend remains absolute. He was the one who spent the last days by her bedside, hearing things she wouldn't tell even her children—especially her children. He writes to me about his accomplishments as a mountaineer. He offers analyses of U.S. presidential elections. He retains a relationship to the spiritual, although I wouldn't call him religious. For confirmation he sent me a Luther Bible. Without ever having had an institutional affiliation (occasionally he has taught a course at the free university) he is the scholar *par excellence.*

You, on the other hand, married a Canadian and moved to Montreal, where my parents first emigrated. The four of you spent a year together as newlyweds, in a climate so cold my mother vowed never to return. *Instead they moved to New York— just for a year, they told themselves.* Then there was the year we lived in London, where you had moved, your husband a foreign correspondent for a Canadian newspaper. My father was employed by the Navy. I am in fourth grade. You and she catch up again, although the children never seem to hit it off. *Your daughter, who settled in England, etches glass windows for the houses of rock stars. Your sons remain in Canada. None of them have married.* You keep trying to convince my brother and me to leave the house by saying (in a Swiss accent my brother mimics repeatedly): "Don't you want to go out on King's Road?" It's the early 1960s, after all. But to no avail.

Eventually you and she have a falling out. You move back to Toronto, which is where I find you after my mother's death.

I come to visit you in that stately house, in an old residential part of the city. Sometimes I sleep on the third floor, sometimes in your study. The Himalayan cat is fed home-grown pot from the movie-reel tin in the TV room. Your color diary, painted in tiny squares of watercolor, hangs on the dining-room wall. The back terrace where we eat on warm summer evenings, holds a woman's head carved in stone (now residing near a flowerbed in Dorset). You take books off the shelves asking me if I have read them, reminding me to read them again. You take me to art galleries where you are acquainted with the owners. You show me articles you have written on contemporary artists, like Christo. You talk to me about my mother.

In many ways you are so different, although I can see why you would have become friends. *You, the daughter of a businessman who went to art school; she the daughter of a doctor who studied law. Both such solid members of the bourgeoisie, although I've always suspected your family had more money.* Although you both married foreigners and spent most of your lives in North America, Switzerland forever followed you in your speech. *When people asked my mother where she was from and she said "Switzerland," the response was often: "Sweden is such a beautiful country."* But you felt at home in your marriage in a way my mother never did. You still share a household with the only spouse you have ever known. *That year in London, I remember watching the fate of the family being decided behind glass doors. My parents sat with my father's secretary, who was pregnant and wanted to marry him.* You also felt at home in America in a way my mother never did. You learned to feel comfortable writing in English. *My mother, toward the end of her life, struggling over the introduction to an anthology of German women writers in translation. The first piece for publication she had ever written in English, it took her forever. And yet she was such a talented writer. She had such a gift for languages.* You have always had your watercolors. A language that speaks without words. A diary that communicates through color and requires a different kind of translation. You always make do, as a freelancer. For her, moving from one job to the next never felt like more than making do.

What would she say, if she knew this is what we were saying about her?

By the time I moved to the Midwest, you had retired to England. To Lyme Regis, of all places. (Where they filmed *The French Lieutenant's Woman.* Where Jane Austen saw the "Granny's teeth" she describes in *Persuasion.*) You put the Himalayan cat in quarantine. You boxed up the color diary, which now hangs in one of the guest rooms. *The house you live in was once a B&B. People still come by to show their fiancées where they spent their childhood summers.* You took all of your books and continue to send me newspaper clippings, the British view of America, American feminism, in particular. Your life hasn't changed much, not as much as your husband's, who still hasn't given up smoking, wonders whether he should join a political club, and continues to garden. The garden with a view of the bay. The cut flowers on the table in my room waiting for my return. The lunches that appear on the patio, carried out on sea-grass trays. *Unlike my mother, you never expect me to help in the kitchen.*

You are always coming up with projects for me to pursue. Usually they involve some form of writing (*even though I have mentioned, albeit shyly, that I have started making paper, that I have learned to bind books*). That's your domain, I suppose. Like these letters. You suggested a series of letters, to different addressees, you thought, when you received the Christmas letter I wrote describing my precipitous entrance into menopause. I remember feeling highly self-conscious about sending that letter to you, writing about aging to someone who is obviously so much older, who has passed through middle age, who has had several close calls with the Angel of Death.

You have also had a hysterectomy and use a patch, which is more commonly prescribed in Europe. *Here they want the estrogen to be absorbed through the liver, if possible, to prevent heart disease.*

At least the stories now being told about menopause are being told by women who have actually been there, whether they supplement this experience by relying on other women who enter their practice seeking medical advice or appear by the thousands in lecture halls in order to have their stories validated. Even the gynecologist is taken by surprise and buys a thinner quilt before she realizes she is having hot flashes. The mother of the wise-woman can barely remember menopause: she finds a box of

Kotex cleaning out the linen closet, realizes she hasn't used them in years, and throws them out.

Every lecture on menopause begins with a definition of the word (the word that refers to an event that can only be recognized as such once it has long passed, i.e., the last menses). Every talk begins by explaining how the female body works, what happens to the hormones during the menstrual cycle. *As though we had forgotten everything we had ever learned in health education. As though we knew nothing about our bodies. What, exactly, did they teach us? Did you remember that we are born with 400,000 eggs, have 200,00 left by puberty and lose 1,001 eggs each cycle, of which there are approximately 400 in a lifetime?*

Two talks in particular discuss menopause in terms of changes, mostly changes that produce symptoms and cause diseases. For the gynecologist the changes are cosmetic—skin loses its thickness, hair appears on the face and fat redistributes itself. For the wise-woman the changes are cosmic, stages in a metamorphosis, from caterpillar to butterfly: (1) needing to be alone (a crone's year, or if financially unfeasible, a crone's moment away, until the hot flash passes), (2) meltdown or the "don't call me mom" stage, and (3) becoming the baby crone, who can't expect to turn into a butterfly until she's sixty. The changes focused on by the gynecologist can be alleviated with estrogen and by resetting one's ideal body weight. This is part of what it means not to be "a passive victim," to "take charge of one's future health and well-being" (so as not to become a burden to the health care system, adding to the $10 billion a year deficit caused by osteoporosis). The changes mentioned by the wise-woman are an attempt to harness the "most radical kind of change," i.e., planetary change, having spent the "best years of one's life as a victim" (of patriarchy). While the gynecologist seeks to preserve femininity as a "sense of well-being" in the face of undesired gender equality ("coronary equality with men," "male pattern obesity"), the wise-woman defends herself against both the

male-controlled medical establishment (which has $3 billion a
year to gain if all menopausal women opt for HRT) and the
feminist doctor who claims that at menopause "the vagina dries
up, one becomes incontinent, one can't have orgasms and the
uterus falls out." Are these differences to be understood in terms
of social class, official vs. unofficial discourses, liberal vs. cultural feminism?

Ultimately they both offer a feminist critique of a previous
conception of menopause as "resignation without compensa-
tion," whether this means insisting on the inclusion of women as
experimental subjects or reclaiming women's own stories about
menopause. They both believe that menopausal women represent
social change agents, as "menopausal boomers" who will re-
define menopause or as postmenopausal women who will change
the world. *How comforting to always be part of the vanguard, the
source of Generation X's envy.* They both argue that this change
should be about women becoming more focused on themselves
("let it awaken in you a need to care for yourself" "don't call
me mom") either as "better consumers of health care needs" or
as more mature crones.

Where of course they completely disagree is over HRT.

There is no answer written anywhere to the question, "Should
I take estrogen?" There are only ideological differences, a battle
waged over the meaning of the word "natural." Natural menopause means turning to herbal allies that come from the earth
(wise-woman). There is nothing natural about menopause if sixty
to one hundred years ago women died between forty and fifty
years of age, i.e., didn't outlive their ovaries (gynecologist). Will
postmenopausal women become a burden to the health care system or are they a limitless source of profit for pharmaceutical
companies? Within a liberal ideology having choices necessarily
means being able to choose not to take hormones; yams and tofu
are said to be a good source of estrogen, but that's all the doctor
knows. Within a medicalized culture one has to recognize those

whose suffering might be alleviated by traditional medicine; the ten percent of all women who have severe symptoms, might benefit from HRT for a short time, the wise woman is willing to concede. The fact that only 15 to 20 percent of menopausal women are on HRT is a sign, for the doctor, that it is not being offered widely enough to patients; for the wise woman, that there is something laughable about the concept of medical noncompliance. *Of course women aren't going to take something that increases their risk for breast cancer.*

If one refuses HRT, one has only oneself to blame, resisting the lure of longevity. *Every now and then a health care provider will agree that we have to die of something. They just haven't agreed on what.* If one takes advantage of it, who will shed tears when one becomes another victim of its little-known side effects? *This is the ultimate meaning of choice under postindustrial capitalism, too many choices, none of them risk-free. The only choice one doesn't have is not to consume: drugs, herbs, ideologies.*

In the meantime, all one can do is assess the severity of one's symptoms, one's potential risk for disease.

"How do you feel?"

A godmother who was chosen by my mother. Who had a falling out with her. Who stepped in when my mother died. Who has nurtured my artistic side.

A fairy godmother? Yes, of sorts.

Occasionally we lapse into Swiss-German. When we do it's usually to make fun of a language whose culture neither of us can take quite seriously *(although from you I would expect more reverence, since your connection is not that of the immigrant's offspring).* And yet it is what binds us to each other, and, ultimately, to my mother.

What is it, exactly, this part you were asked to play, as "godmother"? A mother substitute? A symbolic mother? Hardly a mother "in god." *(You've never been quite that.)*

The final addressee. The one left holding the skin that has been shed as a result of writing these letters.

A recurring dream. I am running too fast on a terrace overlooking a cliff and because the wall is too low I fall over the edge (in one version I am holding my ex's hand). I wake up thinking: how will I know when I am dead, how will I know what death is, if this is only a dream?

A "precipitated" change. A change precipitated by the loss of organs. Premature. Precipitating a reliance on memory marked by a confrontation with mortality, signaling the entrance into middle age. A second baptism?

You ask me how I am.

It's been almost six months.

The hormones have eliminated the hot flashes. I'm able to sleep again, at least five or six hours, uninterruptedly. I continue to suffer from chronic lower back pain. No, it's nothing new. It's just that the pain can't disappear anymore with my periods.

It's been only six months.

I still cry easily. As though I were wearing my emotions on my sleeve.

I still tire quickly. Several hours of social interaction and I feel exhausted, to the bone.

No reserves.

My skin is no longer dry, no longer almost translucent. My frame is no longer as thin, reminiscent of an adolescent boy; my joints are now vocal with every unexpected move.

It this what it feels like to grow old?

And now, if not forever feminine, forever young? I don't think so.

It's been over six months now.

This consistent sense of well-being. This unfamiliar ability, when I am asked how I am, to almost always say "I am doing well." Is it the estrogen? Is it the oatstraw? Is it the contrast to having been so ill? An undiagnosed condition: endometriosis. An undiagnosable condition: PMS. When women my age tell me they are exhausted because they have just gotten their periods, or they had to find another set of clothes because they leaked so badly at work, I feel as if I belong to a different species.

Is this it? Am I done? Will I have done the work of seven years in a year and seven months? Will I be spared what my peers still anticipate, if even that?

What will I be doing, then?

Who will I be doing it with, if not with them?

How will I know?

Chapter 9

Letter to Myself

In the soft darkness that hides the future from the over-curious, I content myself with this; that where I will be will not be where I am. The cities of the interior are vast, do not lie on any map.

Jeanette Winterson, *The Passion*

Who is this addressee?

Who do I think I am writing to?

The one I won't recognize until I have finished addressing her.

The one who exists for as long as there is no other addressee.

The one I can barely remember: racked by menstrual cramps; suffering from PMS symptoms—agoraphobia, chocolate cravings, extreme tearfulness—between temper tantrums and deep despair. Tender breasts, weight fluctuations, fear of insemination. Diaphragms, the day-after-pill, tampons. Painkillers I could not go anywhere without, not on any day of the year, because the fear of not taking one in time produced such paranoia. Ruptured cysts: I thought nothing could be more painful than a UTI, knowing that if the physical pain got any worse, the mind would go. *At some point they become inseparable, then one knows one has lost it.* I never even had an STD or an unwanted pregnancy. By the time I had my first yeast infection, it was (once again) the worst the doctor (who worked for a girl's school) had ever seen.

The feeling that only by ripping off my skin could I escape these fetters I was in.

Then my period would come, and it was like a cloud lifting (what a cliché), like walking on cotton, and with it would disappear my fear of pregnancy and my lower back pain. Now all I had to contend with was menstrual pain, which seemed easy. And if I was lucky, between my period and PMS, if nothing else happened, nothing "real" (the result of an actual life event, like loss or frustration or a sense of failure), I had a week off. Once a month. Every month, for thirty years.

Is she the one I will miss?

How could I?

Yet she is the one I have known most intimately.

The acupuncturist. An improbable addressee. An Israeli, with a Russian name. Shoulder-length black curls and perfectly manicured hands. He is gentle. *He reminds me of my current lover.* He wears artisanal vests and black jeans. He speaks English with a pronounced accent. *The graduate student who sent me to him said he would have a hard time understanding me on the phone.*

Israel, a small country, where something always happens.

Switzerland, a small country, where nothing ever happens.

I look up both in the atlas. Israel is even smaller than Switzerland (how can that be?) with many more inhabitants.

I had never been to an acupuncturist (or a massage therapist, or a physical therapist, or any kind of body worker, except the chiropractor). I had no idea what to expect.

A crush.

A flirtation.

An infatuation.

Like a rerun of adolescence: anticipating my weekly visits; wondering what I was going to wear; my heart palpitations when I arrived, which he would notice and ask me about when he took my pulse. And it's clear that as a fantasy it was mutual *(except that he had a wife and two children, which I only learned about much later, from the graduate student. Except that I was a lesbian, which I told him, not knowing why, right off the bat, when he asked me why I didn't have children.* The nervousness with which we sat next to each other on the wicker settee, while he explained how to take a certain Chinese herb. The meaningful embrace at the end of the session, as a prelude to my departure, once he had touched my arm and I had taken his hand, which he didn't resist, although it made him nervous. The final embrace, I in tears and he responding with audible but inarticulate sounds, signifying pleasure, anticipating loss. Two people in exile: he in a country in whose language he lacked fluency; I in a body whose workings had become unfamiliar.

Two people in transition: I on my way into middle age; he on his way back to Jerusalem.

Male healer; female patient. It forces the man to be the nurturant one; it allows the woman to be taken care of.

A different scene of seduction.

During my first visit, I was surprised by the painless insertion of the needles. *The graduate student had mentioned that of all the acupuncturists she had been to, which were many, his touch was the most delicate. She was dying of breast cancer. She was only thirty-two. She had been my student, until she decided to work with someone else. I couldn't make myself attend her memorial service, several months later.* Except for the one in the ear, the first one. Except for the occasional one in the ankle, which he would always warn me about. "Take a breath," he would say, the last word acquiring several syllables.

I spent my first session in tears, literally sobbing. Was this normal, I wondered? He provided me with plenty of tissues. He was gently reassuring. When I came back he was delighted by how successful it had been. All those pathways unblocked, all that *chi* rerouted, all that circuitry reconnected. My body was finally able to let go of the trauma of surgery. For the first time in months my back felt better. It was like a miracle. How difficult not to fall for someone who is able to relieve so much pain, who is so gentle, so calm.

I spent my last session in tears, determined not to feel sad. I pulled out my handkerchief. He said, "You will be all right." The very day I was going to ask him what he did when he wasn't working (taking the man's lead) he mentioned that he was returning to Israel. After eight months, and a previous summer, in a midsize Midwestern university town, he was going back. He said it was the weather. *The winters were too cold, the air too dry; the summers not warm enough. When my brother went back to Switzerland, he said it was the bread.* The graduate student said it was the "language barrier." He had posted lectures, workshops, at the local food coop to introduce people to acupuncture. He wanted to make it a form of treatment covered by medical insurance, rather than just a form of relaxation. But people didn't come. He had thought about Arizona. After eight years abroad, professional opportunities had opened up in Israel, he said.

Why wouldn't one go home, if one could.

Once he removed and disposed of all the needles, he gave me a massage. The scent of the oil joined the scent of the Chinese herbs already in the room. It was warm from the space heater. It was spring and then summer. A summer remembered for its lack of heatwave. One day when I came and had to wait for the previous patient to finish dressing, he pointed out the double blooms on the flowering crab apple in front of the office building where he rented space from a chiropractor toward whom he seemed to harbor an antagonism. We talked about the partial eclipse we had both experienced that day. The white light. The mysteries of nature, which is what drew him to acupuncture in the first place, the day his brother brought home brochures, when he was still in Tel-Aviv.

Shortly before he left, he changed venues. *That should have been my clue.* This time he shared space with a woman who did acupressure, a friend of his, with a Latina name. On the top floor of a Victorian house, downtown. Decked out in Victoriana: lace curtains, floral pillows, wicker chairs. *Now she too has left for acupuncture school in southern California.* The afternoon I arrived, he was sitting on the landing, behind the railing, reading. He was waiting for me. He watched me as I climbed the stairs before he let me know he was there.

We smiled.

We knew.

We said nothing.

Once when I enumerated all the losses I had shared the last few months (the mothers of three close friends, the brother of my haircutter, the fathers of two other friends) and how each time it reminded me of my own mother's death, he asked how old I had been. *Not a child, but still too young.* He looked as puzzled as when I first said I wasn't a mother. It was something he couldn't understand, like my being a professor. When I said it made me think a lot, these losses, which was good, since I was a professor, he laughed. "A professor," he said, and laughed again.

Both of our desires mediated by the desire for the other person's knowledge. An English professor. The language he wished he could master, speak more fluently, understand more easily. He would ask me to explain idiomatic expressions, such as "being out of sorts." He would ask me to pronounce words again, for instance, "handkerchief," which he had learned from a Beatles' song. For some reason I felt the need to explain further, to expound on what I imagined to be its etymology. "Hanker," I said, meant nothing, and "chief" had nothing to do with the object, its referent. *Analogizing it to the explanation for "rasp/berry" I had once learned in a linguistics class.* A strange word, no doubt Anglo-Saxon. *When I finally looked it up in the dictionary, suspicious that my explanation had relied more on the poetic than the prosaic, and found "scarf for the head," (hand/kerchief), I thought, of course, I know that, and laughed to think that part of being a teacher is pretending to know and hoping that he would soon forget everything I had said. But of course it's always those things that students most remember. False etymologies.*

What was it that I did know? How had it become so valued in this setting, when it was taken for granted or ignored in most others? Either I was to finally own that knowledge, or decide to throw it all away. For a while I wanted to throw it all away, replace it with something new. *As a colleague once put it, when we change, we expect the environment we are in to change with us.* I sent away for information about acupuncture schools, gathered from yoga magazines and acupuncture books, which I began to read religiously. Almost all of the schools were located on either coast, designed for people who lived in cities and continued to work during the day. I finally decided on one in southern California. It included Chinese massage and herbology. Three years. Could I, would I, take that long a leave? I could turn one of my rooms into an office. I could start a practice a few hours a week. I could continue after I retired. Several people had already volunteered to become my patients. One colleague even said, "Acupunture is you. It's like a poststructuralist approach to the body."

Freud has written that there are three impossible professions—educating, healing, and governing. The first two are clearly related. (The last one I have always known to be impossible and therefore have never been interested in.) By becoming a patient, I had come to understand myself as an educator, for the first time. Stripped of my professional identity, I have became a recalcitrant body in pain. *I insisted on a weekly appointment even after the treatments no longer had the cataclysmic effect of my initial visit. I wanted a cure, but short of that I was in search of someone who would mediate between me and my body, someone who would lay hands on my body in an effort to alleviate the pain, in an attempt to give back to me a body I could recognize.* I am admired for something I can't help knowing, namely English, something I have spent my whole life trying to not feel a stranger in. And at this moment I have succeeded. What I know has become desirable. I think about everything else I have learned, imparted to others, will continue to take an interest in. But what does all that matter compared to alleviating someone's pain?

I want to do for others what he has done for me.

We save souls, a colleague likes to remind me. A body in pain but a mind at last/at least mindful of her accomplishments.

Israel, a place I have never seen. *His very last appointment, the one who came after me, a young Jewish man with whom he speaks Hebrew, a language I will never know.* The only place I have never been that I now wish to go to. *A colleague said she would take me the next time she went. She left, precipitously, in search of solace. Next time? she wrote on the back of a postcard I receive from Jerusalem.* I search for images everywhere, on calendars, in advertisements from the tourist bureau, in magazines. Every morning I look to see if there is news. *I have never been interested in the politics of the Middle East. They have always seemed so baroque and my interest could only be belated in that something has been going on for so long. I will never catch up.* I see *Schindler's List,* by myself, since everyone I know has already seen it. I hear Noa, the most popular young singer in Israel, on tour. I order a novel out of a publisher's catalogue about German Jewish musicians who emigrate to Palestine in the 1930s. I insist on a trip to the big city to see the latest Wasserstein play. I buy a pair of shoes made in Israel, in deep blue. One friend says she wouldn't recommend moving there. Another is afraid that I will want to convert.

But it's not about conversion.

It's about compassion. *For weeks I am obsessed by whether or not I am a compassionate person, in what ways my compassion might manifest itself. Or whether I am, once again, the object of someone else's compassion.*

It's about perversion.

It's not about straightening out the crooked. It's about imagining what it would be like to go home, not by changing citizenship, but by remembering the romantic ideal. A hysterectomized woman is different from an infertile or menopausal one, is different from one using some form of birth control. Especially if she is young, which is what people keep telling me I am. There is something about sex being permanently divorced from reproduction, not temporarily, not gradually, but instantly and irrevocably, that, for a woman, cannot be experienced sexually except in relation to another woman. But in no other way in relation to a man, whether that man is freely chosen or has imposed himself through violence. Sex will never again be coupled with the fear of pregnancy, with the psychological and social responsibility of conception, with an unwanted maternity and its irreversible effects. In that sense, the hysterectomized woman has become more like a man. In that sense, to be with a man can be a choice again.

Does this make any sense?

To whom?

Wanting to throw it all overboard, one last time. Nostalgia not for what has been lost, but for the place one will never get to. The language I don't speak, the religion I don't share, a country I have never seen.

And yet it's all so familiar. An effeminate man. Cross-cultural identification. Transgressive desire.

One imagines giving it all up, until one realizes there was so little to give. Which one realizes once there is too much to give away. At which point it all becomes unimaginable.

These feelings that I have one more time. It's not that I've returned to the beginning, which is where I belong. It's not that it's too late, now that I'm no longer young. *People in their late twenties still say "our age," and I wonder, yours or mine.*

I no longer know who she is.

A letter to myself. Is that because that is all I have left or because this is the only way to find out who she is?

I never considered myself straight, even when I had male lovers, even now that I have a male lover.

I have always identified as lesbian, even before I knew the word. Even before I knew any. Even now that the desire is tinged with nostalgia.

How queer.

It's not just about being sexual, even if for the first time I know what that means, without pain, without fear, without misplaced desire.

private & public

It's about independence (a straight woman without a man, outside of marriage, is always considered "single").

It's about being an intellectual (having conversations with men whose desires have been displaced).

It's about being childless (in a way that needs no justification, even as many lesbians are choosing otherwise).

But is she really one?

A letter to myself. Now that I am finally alone, without feeling lonely, I still seek an addressee. Now that I can finally call myself a writer, I still write in the form I first knew. Now that I live in a body that at long last feels like my own, I can finally own what it is that I have always wanted to say.

Who is this addressee?

Who is she now?

Who will she be, down the road, in some other place, on some other map?

"I'm telling you stories. Trust me."

Bibliographic Essay

The kind of writing that I most admire and feel indebted to is that of British feminist cultural studies, a genre that combines autobiography, history, and cultural analysis as a way of coming into writing. In particular this includes Carolyn Steedman's *Landscape for a Good Woman* (Rutgers, 1986), but also Annette Kuhn's *Family Secrets: Acts of Memory and Imagination* (Verso, 1995), from whom I have borrowed the term "memory work."

The memoirs I have been most inspired by include academic memoirs and memoirs written by gay men. Among the former I would include Patricia Williams' *The Alchemy of Race and Rights: Diary of a Law Professor* (Harvard, 1991), which breaks the bounds of legal writing in order to offer astute and compelling observations of American legal and popular culture, and Alice Kaplan's *French Lessons* (University of Chicago, 1993) which considers what it means to live in two languages, having learned one as a foreign language in order to teach it to others. Wayne Koestenbaum combines both genres in *Opera, Homosexuality, and the Mystery of Desire* (Poseiden, 1993), and although I cannot claim to share his interest in opera, I have learned much about cross-gender identification and the reliance of desire on nostalgia. Among gay male memoirs my favorites include Neil Bartlett's *Who Is That Man?* (Serpent's Tail, 1998), which extends British cultural studies to address issues of queerness in its consideration of contemporary London as seen through the lens of Oscar Wilde; Samuel Delany's *The Motion of Light in Water* (Plume, 1988), which takes place in the East Village between 1957 and 1965 and comes to terms with being married, gay, black, and a writer; and Richard Rodriguez's *Days of Obligation: An Argument with My*

Mexican Father (Viking, 1992) which considers what it means to grow up biculturally when the two nations have such differing relations to geography, the nation state, and religion.

Other memoirs I much admire are Susanna Keysen's *Girl, Interrupted* (Vintage, 1993) in terms of the perfection of the prose poem, which focuses on mental illness, and the late Gillian Rose's *Love's Work: A Reckoning with Life* (Schocken Books, 1995), a philosopher's consideration of physical illness and her own dying.

About memoirs, the most interesting book I have encountered, one that includes several bibliographic essays, is William Zinsser, ed., *Inventing the Truth: The Art and Craft of Memoir* (Houghton Mifflin, 1987).

In terms of what is available in bookstores on menopause, there is still not much to recommend. The most popular self-help books are Gail Sheehy's *The Silent Passage: Menopause* (Pocket Books, 1991) and Lonnie Barback's *The Pause: Positive Approaches to Menopause* (Signet, 1993). For a mainstream medical approach to the topic I have found Winnifred Cutler's *Hysterectomy: Before and After* (HarperCollins, 1988) to be just about all there is. Susun Weed's *Menopausal Years: The Wise Woman Way* (Ash Tree Publishing, 1992) offers alternative approaches, although mostly to natural menopause.

Several collections of autobiographical and/or imaginative writings have recently appeared, includng Dena Taylor and Amber Coverdale, eds., *Women of the 14th Moon: Writings on Menopause* (Crossing Press, 1991); *A Certain Age: Reflecting on Menopause* (forewords by Nancy K. Miller and Carolyn G. Heilbrun, Columbia University Press, 1994); and Lynne Taetzsch, ed., *Hot Flashes: Women Writers on the Change of Life* (Faber and Faber, 1995). Germaine Greer's *The Change: Women, Aging, and the Menopause* (Ballantine, 1991) offers a more historical approach to the ideology of menopause, and a consideration of the topic by women in the academy can be found in Joan Callahan, ed. *Menopause: A Midlife Passage* (Indiana, 1993).

The videotapes I discuss are Judith Reichman's *Straight Talk on Menopause* (PBS, 1993) and Susun Weed's *The Menopausal Years* (1993).

The most companionable piece of writing I discovered during recovery proved to be a menopause newsletter entitled *A Friend Indeed*, which is published in Montreal and appears monthly, and can be subscribed to in the United States by writing to P.O. Box 1710, Champlain, NY 12919-1710.

Order Your Own Copy of
This Important Book for Your Personal Library!

A MENOPAUSAL MEMOIR
Letters from Another Climate

_____ in hardbound at $39.95 (ISBN: 0-7890-0296-5)

_____ in softbound at $14.95 (ISBN: 1-56023-919-0)

COST OF BOOKS_____

OUTSIDE USA/CANADA/
MEXICO: ADD 20%_____

POSTAGE & HANDLING_____
(US: $3.00 for first book & $1.25
for each additional book)
Outside US: $4.75 for first book
& $1.75 for each additional book)

SUBTOTAL_____

IN CANADA: ADD 7% GST_____

STATE TAX_____
(NY, OH & MN residents, please
add appropriate local sales tax)

FINAL TOTAL_____
(If paying in Canadian funds,
convert using the current
exchange rate. UNESCO
coupons welcome.)

☐ **BILL ME LATER:** ($5 service charge will be added)
(Bill-me option is good on US/Canada/Mexico orders only;
not good to jobbers, wholesalers, or subscription agencies.)

☐ Check here if billing address is different from
shipping address and attach purchase order and
billing address information.

Signature_____

☐ **PAYMENT ENCLOSED: $**_____

☐ **PLEASE CHARGE TO MY CREDIT CARD.**

☐ Visa   ☐ MasterCard   ☐ AmEx   ☐ Discover
☐ Diners Club
Account #_____

Exp. Date_____

Signature_____

Prices in US dollars and subject to change without notice.

NAME_____

INSTITUTION_____

ADDRESS_____

CITY_____

STATE/ZIP_____

COUNTRY_____ COUNTY (NY residents only)_____

TEL_____ FAX_____

E-MAIL_____
May we use your e-mail address for confirmations and other types of information? ☐ Yes   ☐ No

Order From Your Local Bookstore or Directly From
The Haworth Press, Inc.
10 Alice Street, Binghamton, New York 13904-1580 • USA
TELEPHONE: 1-800-HAWORTH (1-800-429-6784) / Outside US/Canada: (607) 722-5857
FAX: 1-800-895-0582 / Outside US/Canada: (607) 772-6362
E-mail: getinfo@haworth.com
PLEASE PHOTOCOPY THIS FORM FOR YOUR PERSONAL USE.

BOF96